The Soviet Union: The History and Legacy of the USSR from World War I to the End of the Cold War

By Charles River Editors

Vladimir Lenin

About Charles River Editors

Charles River Editors is a boutique digital publishing company, specializing in bringing history back to life with educational and engaging books on a wide range of topics. Keep up to date with our new and free offerings with this 5 second sign up on our weekly mailing list, and visit Our Kindle Author Page to see other recently published Kindle titles.

We make these books for you and always want to know our readers' opinions, so we encourage you to leave reviews and look forward to publishing new and exciting titles each week.

Introduction

President Gerald Ford and Brezhnev

The Soviet Union

For 30 years, much of the West looked on with disdain as the Bolsheviks took power in Russia and created and consolidated the Soviet Union. As bad as Vladimir Lenin seemed in the early 20th century, Joseph Stalin was so much worse that Churchill later remarked of Lenin, "Their worst misfortune was his birth... their next worst his death." Before World War II, Stalin consolidated his position by frequently purging party leaders (most famously Leon Trotsky) and Red Army leaders, executing hundreds of thousands of people at the least. And in one of history's greatest textbook examples of the idea that the enemy of my enemy is my friend, Stalin's Soviet Union allied with Britain and the United States to defeat Hitler in Europe during World War II.

Stalin ruled with an iron fist for nearly 30 years before his death in 1953, which may or may not have been murder, just as Stalin was preparing to conduct another purge. With his death, Soviet strongman and long-time Stalinist Nikita Khrushchev (1894-1971), who had managed to stay a step ahead of Stalin's purges if only because he participated in them, became the Soviet premier.

A barely known figure outside of the Eastern bloc, Khrushchev was derided as a buffoon by one Western diplomat and mocked for his physical appearance by others, but any Western hopes that he would prove a more conciliatory figure than Stalin were quickly snuffed out as the hard-line Khrushchev embraced confrontational stances. In a statement to Western diplomats at the Polish embassy in Moscow, Khruschev famously warned, "We will bury you." And after his first meetings with President John F. Kennedy, Kennedy famously compared Khrushchev's negotiating techniques to his own father's. Even today, one of Khrushchev's most memorable moments is banging his shoe at a United Nations General Assembly meeting in September 1960 while a Filipino delegate was speaking.

Personal histrionics aside, Khrushchev meant business when dealing with the West, especially the United States and its young president, John F. Kennedy. After sensing weakness and a lack of fortitude in Kennedy, Khrushchev made his most audacious and ultimately costly decision by attempting to place nuclear warheads at advanced, offensive bases located in Cuba, right off the American mainland. As it turned out, the Cuban Missile Crisis would show the Kennedy Administration's resolve, force Khrushchev to back down, and ultimately sow the seeds of Khrushchev's fall from power. By the time he died in 1971, he had been declared a non-citizen of the nation he had ruled for nearly 20 years.

Leonid Brezhnev became First Secretary of the Communist Party in the Soviet Union in late 1964 after a plot to oust Khrushchev. Little is remembered in the public imagination about Brezhnev in comparison to Mikhail Gorbachev, Vladimir Lenin, or Joseph Stalin, despite the fact Brezhnev ruled the USSR from 1964-1982, longer than any Soviet leader other than Stalin. In fact, he held power during a tumultuous era that changed the world in remarkable ways, and that era has been favorably remembered by many former Soviet citizens. It marked a period of relative calm and even prosperity after the destruction of World War II and the tensions brought about by Khrushchev. Foremost amongst Brezhnev's achievements would be the détente period in the early 1970s, when the Soviets and Americans came to a number of agreements that reduced Cold War pressures and the alarming threat of nuclear war.

On the other side of the balance sheet, Brezhnev oversaw a malaise in Soviet society that later became known as an era of stagnation during which the Communist Bloc fell far behind the West in terms of economic output and standard of living. His regime also became notorious for its human rights abuses, and Soviet foreign policy in his later years took on some of the character of the earlier American behavior that he had so criticised. Most calamitous of all was the invasion of Afghanistan in 1979.

The Cold War moved into one of its most dangerous phases after Brezhnev's death as both sides deployed nuclear weapons within alarming proximity in Europe. A NATO exercise, "Operation Able Archer," almost led to a Soviet miscalculation, and when the Soviets shot down a South Korean airliner in September 1983, claiming it had strayed into Soviet airspace, the Cold War became very tense indeed.

After going through three elderly leaders in three years, Mikhail Gorbachev was chosen as the new General Secretary at the relatively youg age of 54 in March 1985. Gorbachev hoped to build the Soviet economy to relieve the persistent shortages of consumer goods it faced, which were caused by enormous military spending of the Soviet Union. Gorbachev tried to introduce some economic reforms, but they were blocked by communist hardliners. Gorbachev then came to the belief that the Soviet economy could not improved without political reform as well.

Limited political reforms, such as broadcasting uncensored debates in which politicians openly questioned government policy, backfired when they energized eastern European opposition movements which began to overthrow their communist governments in 1989. Gorbachev was unwilling to reoccupy these eastern European nations and use the Soviet army to put down these revolts.

Inspired by the revolts in Eastern Europe, the small Soviet Baltic republics, which had long chafed under Russian rule, also began to clamor for independence from the Soviet Union. In 1990, Gorbachev allowed non-Communist party politicians to run for office throughout the Soviet Union, and the Communist Party lost to independence candidates in six Soviet republics, including the three Baltic republics. The Baltic republics then declared independence from the Soviet Union.

In comparison with other Soviet leaders, Gorbachev was leader of the USSR for a relatively short period, but the changes that took place under his leadership were monumental, including some that were intended and others that were unforeseen. Gorbachev oversaw the end of the Cold War and the peaceful transition away from communism in Central and Eastern Europe, and he ended the war in Afghanistan and many other proxy conflicts in the developing world. Gorbachev improved relations with the West and developed enough trust with President Ronald Reagan and President George H.W. Bush to decommission thousands of nuclear weapons. He also liberalized the political environment within the Soviet Union itself, increased accountability, and brought in a certain degree of democracy.

Gorbachev was awarded the Nobel Peace Prize for these efforts in 1990, but his regime also left a legacy of turbulence and destruction in its wake. As a result of his policies, many Soviet people rose up against the status quo, demanding national self-determination and reviving old grievances. Gorbachev could not prevent the USSR from disbanding at the end of 1991, leaving much of the country's economy in ruins and nationalist and ethnic conflicts that are still unresolved today. Gorbachev was more popular abroad than he was at home, and in many respects, historians are still debating the costs and benefits of the last Soviet General Secretary's approach.

The Soviet Union: The History and Legacy of the USSR from World War I to the End of the Cold War examines the Communist superpower from its birth to its demise. Along with pictures of important people and places, you will learn about the Soviet Union like never before.

The Soviet Union: The History and Legacy of the USSR from World War I to the End of the Cold War

About Charles River Editors

Introduction

Free Books by Charles River Editors

Discounted Books by Charles River Editors

Radicals

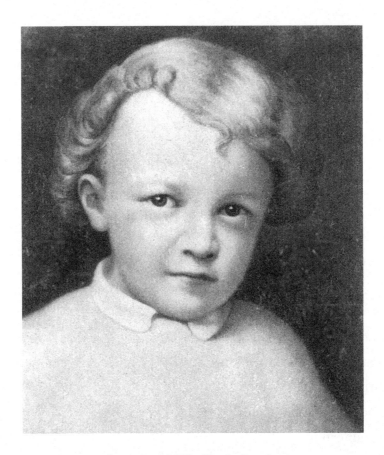

4-year-old Vladimir Lenin

On April 10, 1870, the founder of Russian Communism was born Vladimir Illich Ulyanov to parents Ilya and Maria, who were middle class citizens of the small town of Simbirsk in Russia. Vladimir was their third child, joining Anna and Alexander, and over the next several years, there would be more siblings: Olga, Nikolai, Dmitry and Mariya. With the exception of Nikolai, who died shortly after birth, all his siblings would contribute in some way to the shaping of Lenin's political convictions.

In Lenin's father, we see the first of many ironies that plagued him throughout his life. Though he had hailed from a poor peasant background, Ilya had degrees in both physics and mathematics from the University of Kazan and had taught both at the Penza Institute for the Nobility. By the time "Volodya" (as little Vladimir was known to his family) was born, Ilya had been made the Director of Public Schools for the entire province. During his career, Ilya would supervise the construction of more than 450 schools, built during Russia's 19th century era of modernization, and in recognition of his hard work and success, the Tsar awarded him the Order of St. Vladimir and the position of a hereditary nobleman. Thus, Ilya did what Vladimir would later claim was impossible in Russia: raised himself through ambition and hard work from a peasant to a nobleman. In fact, had there been no revolution, Lenin himself would have inherited his father's title and could have lived out his life as one of the very noblemen whom he had imprisoned and killed.

Ilya

Maria was also well read and well educated. The daughter of a doctor, she grew up in a wealthy family where learning was emphasized for everyone, even the women. She was taught at home by excellent tutors and showed a particular interest in languages and Russian literature. She had a teaching certificate but did not use it after marrying Ilya, though by that time she was fluent in English, French, German, and Russian.

One of the areas of life on which the couple disagreed was religion. Ilya was a member of the Russian Orthodox Church and was very devout, insisting that all his children be baptized and raised in that faith. Maria, on the other hand, was from a Lutheran background and had no particular interest in religion one way or another. It appears that it was her influence, at least in part, that led Lenin towards eventual atheism.

Before then, though, the Ulyanov children would lead relatively happy, well cared-for lives. Their parents were politically neutral, so there was never any threat from the government. Their father went about his work every day while the children went to school at the Simbirsk Gymnasium and Maria cared for the home. The family spent most evenings around the fireplace or dining room table, where Ilya saw to it that his children studied hard so that they would always be star pupils in the schools he supervised. This suited Vladimir just fine, as he was an excellent student and would spend much of his teen years tutoring both his siblings and others in Latin.

The Ulyanovs spent much of their summers with their cousins on Maria's side of the family in a rambling old manor house in Kokushkino. There Vladimir always had someone to play with, whether it was his little sister Olga, with whom he was particularly close, or one of his cousins. On nice days the children tended to play outdoors, retiring when they were tired to rest with a few games of chess.

Sadly, all this came to an end in 1886 when Ilya died of a sudden brain aneurism, when Lenin was just 16. It was around this time that the teenaged Vladimir became an open and avowed atheist. Meanwhile, left a widow with four children still at home, Maria was forced to sell some of the family's property to make ends meet, and to keep her oldest son, Alexander, at St. Petersburg University where he was studying biology. Unfortunately, Alexander might have been better off if he'd had to drop out.

A bright student with a sharp mind, Alexander was not just studying biology; he was also dabbling in ant-Tsarist politics. His favorite authors, Nikolay Chernyshevsky, Dmitry Pisarev and Karl Marx, were all banned on campus because of their diatribes against absolute monarchy. In addition to reading them himself, Alexander also passed these books on to his younger brother, who devoured them with fascination. Vladimir particularly liked Chernyshevsky's *What is to be Done?*

Unfortunately, Alexander and his friends in the People's Will on the university campus were doing more than reading. By 1886 they had decided to take matters into their own hands and attempt to overthrow the government by force. Their first step was to assassinate Tsar Alexander III. As the biology student and nominal scientist in the group, it fell to him to construct a bomb they planned to use to blow up the unpopular monarch. However, their plot was unraveled by authorities, and Alexander was hanged on May 8, 1887.

Vladimir in 1887

The quick deaths in succession of his father and brother made Vladimir the head of the family, but Maria was still determined that he complete his University Education, and Vladimir was happy to comply. After graduating with a gold medal for outstanding performance, he applied to study law at his father's alma mater, Kazan University. At first it seemed that he would not be accepted due to his fraternal connection with an executed political criminal, but some men who had known and respected his father intervened, and young Vladimir was accepted in the fall of 1887.

Perhaps to save money, and perhaps hoping to ensure her second son avoided his brother's fate, Maria rented out the family home in Simbirsk and moved in with Vladimir in Kazan. Of course, this begs the question as to what happened to her three younger children during this time. While that remains unclear, it is likely that as a still-young widow Maria turned to her family for help and sent the children to live with relatives.

Maria

Unfortunately, Maria had good reason to be concerned about Vladimir's politics. Soon after starting his studies in Kazan, Lenin joined the Samara-Simbirsk Council, a banned organization on campus. Nevertheless, the group met in secret, and Vladimir rose quickly among its ranks and was chosen to represent the group at the Zemlyachestvo Council, a left-wing organization intent on bringing back the People's Freedom Party (which had assassinated Tsar Alexander II in 1881). On December 4, 1887, he was arrested during a demonstration and expelled from college. In addition, the Ministry of Internal Affairs ordered that he be sent to Maria's family's home in Kokushkino, where they would continue to monitor his behavior.

However, being banished to a quiet country estate only gave Lenin more time to devote to his increasingly radical thinking. Though it remains unclear how he got the books so far from a large city, he read for hours each day, pouring over every belligerent anti-government tome he could get his hands on. Maria was obviously worried about his illegal pursuits and even went as far as to contact the Interior Minister in 1888 to ask that her son be allowed to leave the country and study elsewhere. Though the Minister was not willing to grant the young hot head that level of freedom, he did agree to allow Lenin to return to Kazan to live with Maria and his younger brother Dmitry in a small house on the Pervaya Gora.

Since birds of a feather tend to flock together, Lenin soon made the acquaintance of a fellow revolutionary, M. P. Chetvergova. She was the lynchpin of a secret circle that was devoted to the study and discussion of the works of Karl Marx. Lenin soon became fascinated with Marxist thought, particularly Marx's seminal *Das Kapital*, in which Marx put forth the idea that capitalism is based on the exploitation of the labor of underpaid workers by the owners of the resources they work on. While the young teen had already been dabbling in revolutionary ideals, Marxism really resonated with Lenin, and he became more and more enmeshed in the plight of the workers against the bourgeoisies.

Marx

Maria, herself a member of the bourgeois that her son was condemning, became more and more concerned. In the hopes of getting him away from the influence of his radical friends, she bought a large country house in Alakaevka, Samara Oblast, where she encouraged her son to become a gentleman farmer and to oversee the surrounding gardens and crops. Instead, Lenin spent his time talking to the peasants and studying their way of life. He became increasingly convinced that they were being oppressed by the local landed gentry, and that their poverty could only be alleviated by a radical change in the social and political structure of Russia.

As winter approached that year, Maria moved the family to Samara, a warmer climate where they would not have to deal with the harshest aspects of the notorious Russian winter. Here Vladimir met A. P. Skylyarenko, a dissident who ran a discussion circle devoted to studying and criticizing the government. Together they committed their lives to the propagation of Marxism in their country and the world.

An excellent scholar who had apparently inherited his mother's gift for languages, Lenin spent much of that winter translating Marx and Friedrich Engels's *The Communist Manifesto* from the original German into Russian. He also studied Georgi Plekhanov, who had founded the Black Repartition movement in 1879. Plekhanov maintained that Russia was at that time entering a period of transition in which it would move from being a feudal system to capitalism. This of course disturbed a Marxist like Lenin, since he saw capitalism as the root of all evil.

Engels

Though Maria understandably worried that Vladimir would suffer the same fate as his older brother, one thing that set Lenin and his friends apart from many other radicals of their time (including his deceased brother) was his belief that random violence and murdering officials was pretty useless in the cause of freedom. When he ran into M.V. Sabunaev in 1889, the two shared several heated arguments over her plans to recruit more members to the People Freedom Party in the hopes that they could disrupt the country with random acts of violence. Nearly 15 years later, Lenin would categorically reject the use of "terror", which he described as "the system of individual political assassinations, as being a method of political struggle which is most inexpedient at the present time, diverting the best forces from the urgent and imperatively necessary work of organization and agitation, destroying contact between the revolutionaries and the masses of the revolutionary classes of the population, and spreading both among the revolutionaries themselves and the population in general utterly distorted ideas of the aims and methods of struggle against the autocracy.

Though he did not appear to be following his brother's path of violence against the government, Maria remained concerned enough about Lenin's activities in 1890 that she persuaded the Russian educational authorities to let her son complete his exams for his college degree. After a few months of study, Lenin graduated from the University of Saint Petersburg with highest honors. However, his family's happiness at this triumph was short lived as word soon arrived that his beloved sister Olga had died of typhoid while he was there. For the rest of his life, Lenin would refer affectionately to the little sister he had bullied into following his every command.

Ioseb Besarionis dze Jughashvili was born the fourth child of Ketevan and Besarion

Jughashvili on December 21, 1879. Though his parents were poor peasants living in Gori, Georgia, he was nonetheless pampered and sheltered during his youth, due to the death in infancy of his three older siblings. By the time he was born, his mother was determined not to lose another child to the grim reaper, so she watched his health carefully and made sure he had the best care she and his father, a boot maker, could provide. She even took up washing in order to have more money to provide better food and clothing for her son.

Ketevan

Besarion

Despite his parents' best efforts, young Joseph suffered health scares in childhood. At the age of seven, Joseph experienced the first major health crisis of his life when he came down with smallpox. Night after night his mother sat by his bedside, bathing his feverish head with cool water and trying to keep him from scratching the virulent pox that covered his little body. While little Joseph did survive the dreaded illness, he was left with permanent scars all over his tiny face. For the rest of his childhood he would be taunted by his young friends with the cruel nickname "pocky." One of the most famous aspects of Stalin's regime was its willingness to doctor photos for political purposes, and that extended to Stalin's personal appearance itself, as he later had photographs altered to make his pockmarks less noticeable. Despite being merely 5'4, Stalin would ensure that he was depicted majestically and appear larger than the "little squirt" President Harry S. Truman would later describe upon meeting him.

In addition to that major health scare, young Joseph had a turbulent first 10 years as a result of his father's failed business. Though they were initially faring well, Besarion became an alcoholic and abused his wife and son. Furthermore, the family moved several times during the first decade of Joseph's life, and the young kid grew up in destitute, tough neighborhoods. Even as a child, Joseph engaged in brawls with other kids, experiences that undoubtedly toughened the man who would later famously state, "Gratitude is a sickness suffered by dogs."

In gratitude for his survival of smallpox, the devoutly Christian Ketevan decided her little boy had to have a religious education. She scrimped, saved and wrangled until she secured him a place in the little school run by their local church in 1888. This enraged Besarion, who wished to have the young kid trained as a cobbler. After one drunken episode in which he assaulted Gori's police chief and smashed the windows of the local tavern, Besarion was ordered to leave town. He did so without his family, leaving Ketevan and Joseph on their own.

While at school, the spoiled little boy had his first experience with order and discipline, including having to speak Russian in the classroom instead of his native Georgian. Nevertheless, he excelled in studies, as well as becoming so accomplished at singing that he often sang at weddings.

Although Joseph was excelling in school, he continued to suffer health problems. By the time he started his schooling, Stalin had suffered an injury to his left arm, brought about possibly by blood poisoning or physical abuse, that left his left arm a couple of inches shorter than his right arm. Though Stalin later gave conflicting accounts of how it happened, it was serious enough to exempt him from military service in World War I.

Then, in 1890, Joseph had his second brush with death when he was run over by a carriage pulled by two large horses. While there was no internal damage, his left arm was severely injured and for a time it seemed he might even lose it. With his mother's careful nursing over a period of months, his arm finally healed, but the care available in their small village was not the same as was available in larger cities, so Joseph was sent to convalesce at Tiflis, which just so happened to be the town Stalin's father had headed to after being ordered out of Gori. As a result, his father all but kidnapped the child and forced him to work as a cobbler, only to have

Ketevan and Gori's religious authorities track Joseph down and take him back. After that, Besarion would never associate with Joseph or his mother again.

J. W. STALIN
Foto 1894

Stalin as a teenager

Because he had always been physically weak, Joseph was accustomed to hours of quiet reading and did well at school, earning a scholarship to the exclusive Tiflis Theological Seminary at the age of 16. While there, Joseph joined Messame Dassy, a secret organization committed to promoting independence for Georgia, and there were also young followers of Karl Marx in the group. This proved to be Stalin's first encounter with the revolutionary socialist ideas brewing in Russia at that time. Stalin continued to read all kinds of literature that had been forbidden, from Victor Hugo's novels to socialist revolutionary material, and he persisted even after being caught and punished on several occasions.

Tiflis Orthodox Theological Seminary, circa 1919

By the time he had completed his first year at the school, Stalin had become an avowed atheist. According to one contemporary, upon reading Darwin's *The Origin of Species*, Stalin remarked, "God's not unjust, he doesn't actually exist. We've been deceived. If God existed, he'd have made the world more just... I'll lend you a book and you'll see."

Four years later, at the age of 20, Stalin was expelled from Tiflis for failure to pay his tuition. However, he had already been in trouble with his superiors for flaunting authority and reading prohibited writings. In fact, the real reason for his dismissal may have been that Stalin was already developing his later legendary leadership skills and had been trying to convert some of his fellow students to Marxist socialism. During his school years, he had insisted that his peers refer to him as "Koba", a Robin Hood like protagonist in Alexander Kazbegi's *The Patricide*, and around the time he left school, Stalin discovered some of the early writings of Vladimir Lenin.

The young student now wished to become a revolutionary.

A number of the influential 20th century Communist revolutionaries shared the trait of being publicly known and known to posterity mainly by their pseudonyms. Perhaps the most famous example is Ernesto Guevara de la Serna, the glamorous guerrilla who is known to most as Che Guevara, a nickname that initially referred to his status as an Argentine among Cubans ("Che" is popular slang for an Argentine). The "Big Three" of the Russian Revolution are also remembered by names originally adopted when they were clandestine revolutionaries: Vladimir Ilyich Ulyanov became Lenin, apparently after the Lena River; Joseph Vissarionovich Dzugashvilii became Stalin, "the man of steel"; and Lev Davidovich Bronshtein became Trotsky.

8 year old Lev

Trotsky was apparently the surname of a jailer during Lev's early stint as a political prisoner. Bronshtein had written articles under several different pseudonyms when he was an exiled radical, but Trotsky was the name that stuck. Today, his real name is barely remembered.

His parents, David and Anna, were prosperous Jewish farmers in a rural region of what is now the Ukraine. They were assimilated Jews in the sense that they spoke Russian and Ukrainian at home, and they were largely unobservant when it came to religious practice. Assimilation could only go so far, however; the Tsarist governments varied in the degree of persecution and hostility they directed toward Jews in their territories, but the threat of pogroms was never far away.

In the wake of the assassination of Tsar Alexander II in 1881, falsely blamed on Jews, there were massacres of Jewish populations with tacit or explicit government encouragement throughout Russia and the Ukraine. This was the first decade of Trotsky's life, so it's safe to assume that it left some impression on him. Given the pogroms, it is not surprising that many Jews of Trotsky's generation became involved in anti-Tsarist revolutionary movements. Moreover, they had little attachment to the old Russian order, which was founded on a xenophobic religious nationalism that frequently singled out Jews for both violent attacks and legal harassment. The Bronshteins, however, were comfortable and politically uninvolved, and it is not clear to what degree their son's political ideology had developed when he left home for the city of Odessa.

Tsar Alexander II

In Odessa, Lev Davidovich lived with members of his mother's family, people of cosmopolitan and liberal leanings. There he attended a school that had been modeled on the German *Gymnasium* (for more Western-oriented Russians of the period, German models of education, science, and intellectual life were influential). A major port on the Black Sea and the fourth largest city in the Russian Empire, Odessa was an unusually international city with an openness to the world unusual in the more interior regions of the Empire. Its population included Jews, Armenians, Georgians, Persians, Arabs, Greeks, and Italians, along with French, German, and English merchants. At times, the merchants and Jews comprised a third of the total population. For a revolutionary leader who would later become a tireless international traveler (though not always by choice), a veteran of exile, and an advocate of internationalism, Odessa was an understandably formative environment for a teenager. Odessa was also home to a large urban working class receptive to radical political movements, and it subsequently became legendary because of a workers' and sailors' revolt in support of the Revolution of 1905. The rebels were massacred by Tsarist forces in an incident later made famous in revolutionary director Sergei Eisenstein's 1925 film *The Battleship Potemkin.*

In 1896, Lev moved to the city of Nikolayev, another Black Sea port and major shipbuilding center, to continue his education. It was in this center of both student and working class radicalism that he first became immersed in the political ferment of the period. His first affiliations seem to have been with the Narodnik movement, a highly influential local Russian variety of revolutionary populism. The Narodniks idealized the Russian peasant class as the key to political revolution in Russia. They believed that traditional social life in the Russian countryside and village had been essentially communalistic in orientation, and that the Russian path toward socialism lay in awakening the poor rural masses as a revolutionary class to overthrow the Tsarist order.

The Narodniks' most spectacular achievement was the assassination of Tsar Alexander II in 1881, but their success also led to a major campaign of police repression and censorship that weakened the movement. At the same time, the Narodniks had little success in generating popular support among the population they hoped would spearhead the general revolt against Tsarism, due in large part to the fact they were mainly urban middle-class and upper-class students,.

Lev in 1897

Given his Jewish origins and his many years spent in the urban and cosmopolitan Odessa, it is not surprising that Lev would ultimately be drawn away from Narodnism and toward Marxism. Marxism was an ideology of international orientation premised on the revolutionary potential of the urban working class as a result of the contradictions of the urban capitalist order. The Black Sea coast, with its manufacturing and shipping industries, was home to a large working class that the Marxist student factions in which Lev became involved viewed as an emerging revolutionary force in Russian society. Marxism was a theory fixated on the transformative power of capitalist networks of industry and manufacture, and the tendency of capitalism to engender social conflicts and contradictions that could only be resolved through a revolution that transferred the means of production to the workers themselves. Trotsky was in a place where such a perspective must have seemed very relevant, and he immediately began to act on his convictions.

Though always of an intellectual and theoretical disposition, Lev neglected his studies of mathematics and threw himself into writing for clandestine publications, circulating pamphlets, and organizing secret revolutionary organizations in Nikolayev and Odessa under the name of the South Russian Workers Union. This was exceedingly dangerous. In the wake of the assassination of Alexander II, the Russian police had begun to closely monitor all self-proclaimed radical groups and inflict harsh punishments on anyone they caught involved in anti-government organizations and activities.

When Lev and a number of his companions in the Workers Union were arrested in 1898, they had done little to put their ideas into action other than hold secret meetings and circulate pamphlets, but their incendiary publications and revolutionary intentions were enough to land them immediately in jail. Ironically, imprisonment seems to have had the effect of consolidating the convictions of many young Russian radicals, thus confirming their belief that revolution was the only way forward. Lev spent two years in jail in Odessa awaiting his sentence, and then found himself sentenced to exile and confinement in the same remote and harsh reaches of Siberia where Stalin would later build up an unparalleled network of prison camps. It was during his long imprisonment that he met and married his first wife, fellow radical Alexandra Sokolovskaya, with whom he had two children.

Alexandra, Lev (right), and Alexandra's brothers in 1897

It was also during this period that Lev widely read Marxist philosophy and theory, and he soon came into contact with those who would become his comrades in arms in revolution. Revolution would come sooner than most of them could anticipate.

Trotsky's writings even in 1901 displayed his dual senses of both revolution and optimism. In one 1901 work, he wrote:

"If I were one of the celestial bodies, I would look with complete detachment upon this miserable ball of dust and dirt ... I would shine upon the good and the evil alike ... But I am a man. World history which to you, dispassionate gobbler of science, to you, book-keeper of eternity, seems only a negligible moment in the balance of time, is to me everything! As long as I breathe, I shall fight for the future, that radiant future in which man, strong and beautiful, will become master of the drifting stream of his history and will direct it towards the boundless horizon of beauty, joy, and happiness!

The nineteenth century has in many ways satisfied and has in even more ways deceived the hopes of the optimist ... It has compelled him to transfer most of his hopes to twentieth century. Whenever the optimist was confronted by an atrocious fact, he exclaimed: What, and this can happen on the threshold of the twentieth century! When he drew wonderful pictured of the harmonious future, he placed them in the twentieth century.

And now that century has come! What has it brought with it from the outset?

In France – the poisonous foam of racial hatred; in Austria – nationalist strife ...; in South Africa – the agony of a tiny people, which is being murdered by a colossus; on the 'free' island itself – triumphant hymns to the victorious greed of jingoist jobbers; dramatic 'complications' in the east; rebellions of starving popular masses in Italy, Bulgaria, Romania ... Hatred and murder, famine and blood ..."

With his certification to practice law now firmly under his belt, Lenin returned to Samara and, in January of 1892, took a job as the legal assistant for a member of the regional court. For a man who was becoming gradually more committed to radically changing the nature of Russian government, it should come as no surprise that working for the government was not to his liking. As a result, he soon left to work for A.N. Khardin, a local lawyer whose practice was made up primarily of cases concerning peasants and other similarly needy people.

In spite of his new job, Lenin remained more interested in politics than the law and spent most of his evenings meeting with one or more of his fellow members in Skylarenko's political club. There they talked into the late hours of the night about the ideals of Karl Marx and how they could be applied to the problems facing the Russian people. Lenin became obsessed with collecting information and statistics about the Russian people that would support Marx's ideals about political and economic change.

Lenin gathered together his findings and presented them in a paper he submitted to the Russian Thought in 1893, but they refused to publish his work as it was written. While that work would not see the light of day again until a few years after his death, a few months later Lenin reproduced his research into a book called *On the So-Called Market Question*. In it he summed up his understanding of the plight of the peasants within the context of developing Russian capitalism:

"But only the prosperous peasant can enlarge his crop area, the one who has seed for sowing, and a sufficient quantity of livestock and implements. Such peasants (and they, as we know, are the minority) do, indeed, extend their crop areas and expand their farming to such an extent that they cannot cope with it without the aid of hired laborers. The majority of peasants, however, are quite unable to meet their need for money by expanding their farming, for they have no stocks, or sufficient means of production. Such a peasant, in order to obtain money, seeks "outside employments," i.e., takes his labor-power and not his product to the market. Naturally, work away from home entails a further decline in farming, and in the end the peasant leases his allotment to a rich fellow community member, who rounds off his farm and, of course, does not himself consume the product of the rented allotment, but sends it to the market. We get the "impoverishment of the people," the growth of capitalism and the expansion of the market. But that is not all. Our rich peasant, fully occupied by his extended farming, can no longer produce as hitherto for his own needs, let us say footwear: it is more advantageous for him to buy it. As to the impoverished peasant, he, too, has to buy footwear; he cannot produce it on his farm for the simple reason that he no longer has one. There arises a demand for footwear and a supply of grain, produced in abundance by the enterprising peasant, who touches the soul of Mr. V. V. with the progressive trend of his farming. The neighboring handicraft footwear-makers find themselves in the same position as the agriculturists just described: to buy grain, of which the declining farm yields too little, production must be expanded. Again, of course, production is expanded only by the handicraftsman who has savings, i.e., the representative of the minority; he is able to hire workers, or give work out to poor peasants to be done at home. The members of the majority of handicraftsmen, however, cannot even think of enlarging their workshops: they are glad to "get work" from the moneyed buyer-up, i.e., to find a purchaser of their only commodity—their labor-power. Again we get the impoverishment of the people, the growth of capitalism and the expansion of the market; a new impetus is given to the further development and intensification of the social division of labor."

Having arrived at his personal conclusions about what needed to be done Lenin returned to St. Petersburg, where he got a job assisting lawyer M.F. Volenstein. There he joined S.I.

Radchenko's radical group of "social democratic" students from the local Technical Institute, and, like in previous clubs, Lenin rapidly rose through the ranks. Inspired by the Marxist Social Democratic Party in Germany, they were thrilled to have the popular Lenin as a part of their group and chose him in January of 1894 to secretly debate author V.P. Vorontsov, known for his popular political tome *The Fate of Capitalism in Russia*. Unfortunately, the meeting was not entirely secret. A police officer was sent to monitor their talks and, when he reported what he had heard, the government realized that their old friend Lenin was at it again and stepped up their surveillance of his activities.

It was also around this time that Lenin had met Nadya Krupskaya, a schoolteacher who shared his Marxist leanings and eventually became his wife. She in turn introduced him to other members of her circle of socialist friends who regularly met on Sunday evenings to discuss politics, economics and other related topics. Though he was only in his 20s, Lenin's appearance surprised Nadya's friends, and they gave him the partially affectionate nickname of "old man." At the same time, though, they greatly respected his ideas and soon made him their discussion leader. With their help, he published "What the 'Friends of the People' Are and How They Fight the Social-Democrats," a political tract aimed at exposing those who opposed the political reforms of he and his friends. Now older and becoming ever more cautious, he published it under the pseudonym of Nikolai Petrovich, which he had adopted to avoid police attention.

Nadya

Lenin's writing brought him in conflict with more than just the police, however; he also had problems with the Socialist-Revolutionary Party over what role the peasantry should play in their plans for a new Russia. The SRP saw the peasants as a force to be reckoned with, since they outnumbered the proletariat by 75 to 1. On the other hand, Lenin and his fellow Marxists did not trust the farmers and small land owners, who they saw as simply being small-scale capitalists and part of the problem rather than the solution. In their minds, the future of the revolution lay in an uprising by the proletariat. At the time, the SRP's political inspiration was being provided by the writings of Marxist Georgi Plekhanov, who wrote under the pseudonym "Narodnaya Volga," the last name of the nom de guerre provided by Russia's famous river. It is assumed that when Vladimir used the nom de guerre Lenin for the first time in December 1901, it was a reference to the River Lena and thus an imitation of Plekhanov's pseudonym.

Plekhanov

Hoping to solidify relations between the Russian socialists and those of the rest of Europe, Lenin spent the next several years travelling to several other countries promoting his ideas. Perhaps hoping that being away from Russia would keep him out of jail, Maria financed much of his travel. Lenin first went to Switzerland where, in 1895, he met with several members of the Liberation Labor party. While in Geneva, he was able to meet with the organizer of the Emancipation of Labor Party, who encouraged Lenin to reconsider his perspective on the role of the bourgeoisie in his future plans. From there he went to Zurich, then Paris, where he met with members of the Paris Commune of 1871, before returning to Switzerland and resting in a popular health spa. Then he went on to Berlin, where he spent six weeks studying and meeting with socialist leaders.

Lenin returned to Russia in 1895, his head filled with new ideas and his bags with illegal books and pamphlets. When the workers at St. Petersburg's Thornton textile mill went on strike, Lenin and his followers were there passing out tracts and urging them on. This, along with his latest publication, "The Worker's Cause", proved to be the final straw for the Russian government. Lenin was arrested along with 40 of his fellow activists.

Lenin's 1895 police mugshot

Lenin denied that he had done anything wrong, but was imprisoned in the House of Preliminary Detention while the government put together its case against him. Though Maria and his siblings attempted to intervene on his behalf, he was not granted bail and thus remained in jail during the year leading up to his trial. Lenin was, however, allowed paper and pens, which allowed him to spend most of his time writing on his new favorite topic, class consciousness. By the time he was sentenced, he had completed "Draft and Explanation of a Programme for the Social Democratic Party" and had started writing "The Development of Capitalism in Russia", an attack on the platform of the SRP that he would finish in exile .

In February, 1897, Lenin and his fellow political prisoners were sentenced, without trial, to three years in Siberia. In a surprising show of compassion, the government allowed him a few days of freedom before his departure. Lenin spent this time catching up on the changes that had happened in the Social-Democratic Party during his absence. The most significant of these was that it was now known as the League of Struggle for the Emancipation of the Working Class. Also, with so many of its leader in prison, the common workers had risen to positions of authority, to Lenin's dubious satisfaction.

When he left St. Petersburg for the treacherous 11 hour trip to Shushenskyoye, his mind was no doubt full of politics and plans for the future. However, he likely also regretted leaving behind Nadya Krupskaya, with whom he was romantically involved. However, their parting would not be forever; instead, she joined him in his exile in 1898 after being sentenced to Siberia herself for helping to organize a strike in August of 1896. Ironically, the two atheists were married to each other in a church on July 10, 1898.

As he had in the past, Lenin spent his time in exile reading, studying and writing. He published The Tasks of Russian Social Democrats, in which he concluded:

"Russian Social-Democracy is still faced with an enormous, almost untouched field of work. The awakening of the Russian working class, its spontaneous striving for knowledge, organisation, socialism, for the struggle against its exploiters and oppressors becomes more widespread, more strikingly apparent every day. The enormous progress made by Russian capitalism in recent times is a guarantee that the working-class movement will grow uninterruptedly in breadth and depth. We are apparently now passing through the period in the capitalist cycle when industry is "prospering," when business is brisk, when the factories are working at full capacity and when countless new factories, new enterprises, joint-stock companies, railway enterprises, etc., etc., are springing up like mushrooms. One need not be a prophet to foretell the inevitable and fairly sharp crash that is bound to succeed this period of industrial "prosperity." This crash will ruin masses of small owners, will throw masses of workers into the ranks of the unemployed, and will thus confront all the workers in an acute form with the problems of socialism and democracy which have long faced every class-conscious, every thinking worker. Russian Social-Democrats must see to it that when this crash comes the Russian proletariat is more class-conscious, more united, able to understand the tasks of the Russian working class, capable of putting up resistance to the capitalist class—which is now reaping huge profits and always strives to burden the workers with the losses—and capable of leading Russian democracy in a decisive struggle against the police autocracy, which binds and fetters the Russian workers and the whole of the Russian people."

In addition, Lenin wrote pamphlets and shorter pieces for socialist journals. Then, with Nadya's help, he also translated *The Theory and Practice of Trade Unionism* by Sidney and Beatrice Webb from English into Russian.

When Lenin was released in 1900 he had to leave Nadya behind to finish serving her sentence.

He traveled with his new colleague, Jewish socialist Jules Martov, to Geneva. There they met with one of their heroes, Georgi Plekhanov, the author of *The Development of the Monist View of History*. Operating under his well known pseudonym, Plekhanov was considered to be one of the founders of Russian Marxism, and he had fled Russia for Switzerland after his writings became too unpopular. However, much to Lenin's disappointment, Plekhanov proved very difficult to work with. The older man was suspicious of Lenin, seeing him as a young upstart who wanted to take control of his life's work. He was also very anti-Semitic, and soon offended Martov with his outspoken and rude remarks. Of course, Plekhanov was hardly the only anti-Semitic Russian, which was a source of consternation to Lenin throughout his life. Lenin would later write, "It is not the Jews who are the enemies of the working people. The enemies of the workers are the capitalists of all countries. Among the Jews there are working people, and they form the majority. They are our brothers, who, like us, are oppressed by capital; they are our comrades in the struggle for socialism…Shame on those who foment hatred towards the Jews…"

Copy of the first edition of Iskra

   Though the men remained members of the Liberation of Labor, they decided to begin publishing that new paper, Iskra, in Germany so that Plekhanov could not get his hands on it. Iskra would soon become the official paper of the Social Democratic Labour Party, formed with the intent gather the scattered social revolutionary groups under its one umbrella organization in the hopes of overthrowing the Russian government. Operating for more than 50 years, many of them illegally and underground, Iskra would prove to be one of Lenin's crowning achievements. While he had to secretly smuggle copies into Russia, he was still able to attract some of the finest minds in European socialism to write for the paper. Among these were Rosa Luxemburg from Poland and one of Lenin's fellow Russians.

Luxemburg

While Trotsky was in prison in Odessa, the Russian Social Democratic Labor Party was founded. While he was obviously blocked from direct participation in the formation of the party, he was able to get word of its first congress and follow its developments from afar. It was the moment Russian Marxists had been waiting for: the founding of a major movement that represented and pursued their agenda.

Obviously, the Tsarist police worked hard to strangle the infant movement in its cradle. The leaders who were not quickly arrested and exiled were wise enough to go into exile themselves. Many of the party members formed a core group in London and began publishing the newspaper *Iskra* ("Spark"), whose editorial board included the young Vladimir Ulyanov (Lenin) and the elder statesman of Russian Marxism, Georgi Plekhanov, who had been personally acquainted with Friedrich Engels himself. Plekhanov had been in exile for decades, while Ulyanov (Lenin) and Julius Martov, another influential editor, were of about the same generation as Trotsky and had only recently fled police persecution in Russia.

It was only two years into his Siberian exile that Lev Davidovich Bronshtein successfully fled the country with forged papers identifying him as Leon Trotsky, which at that point became his primary surname for the rest of his life. He left behind his young wife and their two baby daughters, with whom he would never live again. He and Alexandra divorced, and their children were raised partly by the Bronshteins in the Ukraine after leaving Siberia. In essence, Trotsky made a decisive break with his life at the exact same moment that took on an adopted name. By the time he returned to Russia, nothing would be the same, least of all his own position there. He left in 1902 as an obscure exiled radical, but he would return as a leader at the vanguard of a surging revolutionary movement, with Tsarism apparently breathing its last breaths.

Not surprisingly, Trotsky's destination was London, where he was quickly absorbed into the circle around *Iskra*. Trotsky began by publishing numerous articles under the *nom de plume* Pero. Although he may have imagined he would find a united front of like-minded revolutionaries, he soon found that the London community of radical Russian exiles was actually fractured along generational and ideological lines. In fact, the rifts that would turn the early Soviet Union into a bloody theater of factionalism were already taking shape. Lenin and Martov, who saw in the young newcomer a like-minded man of similar age and experiences, were eager to enlist his support for their more action-oriented group. In March 1903, Lenin wrote:

> "I suggest to all the members of the editorial board that they co-opt 'Pero' as a member of the board on the same basis as other members. [...] We very much need a seventh member, both as a convenience in voting (six being an even number), and as an addition to our forces. 'Pero' has been contributing to every issue for several months now; he works in general most energetically for the Iskra; he gives lectures (in which he has been very successful). In the section of articles and notes on the events of the day, he will not only be very useful, but absolutely necessary. Unquestionably a man of rare abilities, he has conviction and energy, and he will go much farther."

However, when Lenin and Martov attempted to make Trotsky part of the editorial board of *Iskra*, the move was blocked by Plekhanov.

In order to understand the conflicts that divided the Russian exile community, it is important to consider the difficulty of applying Marxist revolutionary theory to the Russian context. Marx and Engels had written the *Communist Manifesto* in the years leading up to the European Revolutions of 1848, a series of revolts that shook the countries of Western Europe with a great deal of involvement from the growing industrial working class. For Marx, communist revolution was a necessary consequence of the contradictions created by industrialization and the rise of the middle class or bourgeoisie, which itself had overthrown the rule of the *ancien régime* and installed electoral democratic government by male property owners in varying degrees across Western Europe. Marx and Engels argued that the industrial working class, whose labor fueled the growing wealth of the bourgeoisie, did not benefit from the bourgeois freedoms achieved by the French Revolution and like-minded liberal reforms. To them, the working class' "freedom" was merely a freedom to sell their labor, which indentured them to the propertied classes. As industrialization and commerce spread, Marx and Engels argued, the class of dispossessed workers would grow and eventually demand its own liberation in the form of control of the means of production or machinery of industry.

While these prescriptions were understood to ultimately apply to the world as a whole, the obvious hotbeds of revolution in Marxist theory should have been northern England and the Rhine Valley of northwestern Germany, the most industrialized and proletarianized regions of Europe. But things did not unfold that way. Influential socialist parties did emerge in those places, but for the most part they found success by demanding reform through the "bourgeois" political system. While Marx and Engels took it for granted that the bourgeois would not give up control or power, instead of becoming more repressive and reactionary in response to the burgeoning demands for workers' rights, the bourgeois in the Rhine Valley and northern England saw fit to accommodate some of the demands of the working class. By being more compromising, they reduced the potential for the kind of revolutionary explosion predicted by Marx and Engels.

At the time that Trotsky and his fellow Russians were plotting revolution in London, the evidence that history had not followed Marx's prophesies to the letter was clear enough to see, but the question of exactly how Marxists should respond to these developments was a major source of strife. This was especially true when it came to the vexing problem of revolution in a largely rural country like Russia, which had not even undergone a bourgeois liberal revolution yet.

In light of the Marxist perspectives just discussed, there were two major questions those who sought revolution in Russia had to confront. First, how quickly could Russia undergo a full-scale communist revolution when it had not yet thoroughly undergone the processes of industrialization, urbanization, and liberal reform that Marx had viewed as essential precursors to the proletarian revolution? There were pockets of advanced industrial development in Russia, including places along the Black Sea coast where Trotsky had cut his political teeth, but for the most part it was a traditional rural country that far more resembled the pre-revolutionary French *ancien régime* than the modern industrial cities Marx had seen as ripe for communist revolt. Did Russia first need to undergo a bourgeois liberal revolution and a period of industrialization before Marxism could even become a viable political philosophy there?

Plekhanov was already in disagreement with Lenin and Martov on this issue by the time Trotsky arrived in London. Plekhanov was more orthodox in the sense that he believed a bourgeois revolution and a period of liberal rule, commercial liberalization, and industrialization were necessary precursors to any movement toward communism. In this account of things, the role of Marxists should be to allow liberal reformers to move history forward in a progressive direction and to help organize the growing working class. Naturally, the younger generation was less content to sit on their hands; Lenin and Martov thought Plekhanov's gradualist approach was out of touch with the realities of contemporary Russia, where they had seen the seeds of radical revolt everywhere. On top of that, they knew as well as anyone that the Tsarist regime was more reactionary and entrenched than ever.

However, while Lenin and Martov shared an impatience for the doctrinaire Marxist approaches of their elders, the two were divided over how to make their revolution happen. Should Russian Marxists attempt to bring about change by democratic means in broad coalition with other progressive groups, or should they make use of violent and secretive methods closer to those of the Narodniks and other Russian populist and anarchist groups? It was on this question, particularly acute in a period in which many European socialist parties were operating successfully within democratic systems, that the fateful Bolshevik and Menshevik factions were initially created. The Mensheviks, who followed Martov's thinking, proposed a broad-based, inclusive party open to democratic processes but generally representative of workers' interests and causes.

Martov

Lenin's Bolsheviks, in contrast, emphasized a small and strictly disciplined party organization that was tightly controlled by professional revolutionaries who could lead and orchestrate all action. Trotsky was critical of Lenin's path, and he prophetically wrote at the time, "Lenin's methods lead to this: the party organization substitutes itself for the party, the central committee substitutes itself for the organization, and, finally, a 'dictator' substitutes himself for the central committee. ... The party must seek the guarantee of its stability in its own base, in an active and self-reliant proletariat, and not in its top caucus ... which the revolution may suddenly sweep away with its wing."

The conflicts came to a head at the congress of the Social Democratic Labor Party in London in 1903, with Trotsky originally siding with Martov and the Mensheviks but later declaring himself independent of the key factions. But the more Trotsky attempted to bridge the differences between the rivals, the more he found himself subject to mistrust from members of both groups. While he would ultimately and decisively throw his lot in with Lenin, Trotsky's failure to become a Bolshevik in this early period would much later be seized upon by his political enemies as evidence of his disloyalty and his unauthentic commitment to Lenin's agenda within the Soviet Union.

It was at about this time that the former Ulyanov took the name Lenin as his official nom de guerre. Nadya was also released from Siberia and joined her husband in Munich, where she worked as his personal secretary and helped produce Iskra. In 1903 he wrote To the Village Poor, in which he conceded the Social Revolutionary Party's point about the importance of the peasant population to the political future of Russia. Thus in this pamphlet he appealed to them to rise up against the Russian aristocracy and join the socialist cause.

Rosa Luxemburg, one of the early writers for Iskra, soon spotted a flaw in Lenin's plan. She criticized his plan for a centralized government that would place all the power of lawmaking in the hands of a few intellectually superior leaders. She concluded:

"In general, it is rigorous, despotic centralism that is preferred by opportunist intellectuals at a time when the revolutionary elements among the workers still lack cohesion and the movement is groping its way, as is the case now in Russia. In a later phase, under a parliamentary regime and in connection with a strong labor party, the opportunist tendencies of the intellectuals express themselves in an inclination toward "decentralization." If we assume the viewpoint claimed as his own by Lenin and we fear the influence of intellectuals in the proletarian movement, we can conceive of no greater danger to the Russian party than Lenin's plan of organization. Nothing will more surely enslave a young labor movement to an intellectual elite hungry for power than this bureaucratic straightjacket, which will immobilize the movement and turn it into an automaton manipulated by a Central Committee. On the other hand there is no more effective guarantee against opportunist intrigue and personal ambition than the independent revolutionary action of the proletariat, as a result of which the workers acquire the sense of political responsibility and self-reliance. What is today only a phantom haunting Lenin's imagination may become reality tomorrow."

Meanwhile, in *The Proletariat and the Revolution* (1904), Trotsky wrote about the importance of revolutionary action, even if it doesn't take a visibly militant form:

"The proletariat must not only conduct a revolutionary propaganda. The proletariat itself must move towards a revolution.

To move towards a revolution does not necessarily mean to fix a date for an insurrection and to prepare for that day. You never can fix a day and an hour for a revolution. The people have never made a revolution by command.

What can be done is, in view of the fatally impending catastrophe, to choose the most appropriate positions, to arm and inspire the masses with a revolutionary slogan, to lead simultaneously all the reserves into the field of battle, to make them practice in the art of fighting, to keep them ready under arms, – and to send an alarm all over the lines when the time has arrived.

Would that mean a series of exercises only, and not a decisive combat with the enemy forces? Would that be mere manoeuvers, and not a street revolution?

Yes, that would be mere manoeuvers. There is a difference, however, between revolutionary and military manoeuvers. Our preparations can turn, at any time and independent of our will, into a real battle which would decide the long drawn revolutionary war. Not only can it be so, it must be. This is vouched for by the acuteness of the present political situation which holds in its depths a tremendous amount of revolutionary explosives.

At what time mere manoeuvers would turn into a real battle, depends upon the volume and the revolutionary compactness of the masses, upon the atmosphere of popular sympathy which surrounds them and upon the attitude of the troops which the government moves against the people."

At the same time, Trotsky began to dedicate himself as early as 1904 to elaborating what would become his major contribution to Marxist thought: the theory of permanent revolution. The theory of permanent revolution was an attempt to account for how socialism could be achieved in a so-called "backwards" country like Russia, which had not reached the level of capitalist development presented by Marx as necessary for the emergence of a proletarian revolutionary movement. He wrote, "It is our interest and our task to make the revolution permanent until all the more or less propertied classes have been driven from their ruling positions, until the proletariat has conquered state power and until the association of the proletarians has progressed sufficiently far – not only in one country but in all the leading countries of the world – that competition between the proletarians of these countries ceases and at least the decisive forces of production are concentrated in the hands of the workers. ... Their battle-cry must be: 'The Permanent Revolution'."

While Trotsky certainly sided with Lenin and Martov on the need for immediate action, his initial refusal to throw in his lot with either the Bolsheviks or the Mensheviks was in part determined by his sense that neither group had developed a sound theoretical account of how revolution would in fact come about in Russia. Neither had developed an alternative to the notion that Russia would need to undergo a bourgeois liberal revolution, followed by a period of democratic rule and industrialization, before it could move toward the stage of communist revolution. Permanent revolution was supposed to be an alternative to this "two-stage" theory of political development.

Trotsky, initially in collaboration with fellow Russian exile Alexander Parvus, developed permanent revolution out of some scattered remarks by Marx and Engels that make use of this phrase to refer to the permanently oppositional status of proletarian movements. The key claim of Trotsky's and Parvus's theory was that the Russian bourgeoisie itself was too perennially weak and ineffectual to move the country politically toward the kind of liberal reforms achieved in Western Europe a century earlier. Industrialization in Russia had proceeded to generate a large proletariat through much of the country in advance of any recognizable political liberalization. Given the weakness of the Russian bourgeoisie and the retrenched power of the reactionary Tsarist state, it would fall to the proletariat, in collaboration with the dispossessed rural peasantry, to spearhead any and all political reform. But since the means of production would need to undergo a prolonged development in order to achieve the degree of productivity necessary for an advanced industrial economy, the revolutionary classes would have to oversee a period of "permanent revolution", in which the country would progress toward the adequate conditions for the genuine development of socialism. At the same time, the revolution would have to permanently expand outward in order to foster alliances internationally that would counterbalance the inevitable resurgence of reactionary enemies.

There were significant developments in Trotsky's personal life during his London years as well. After his divorce from Alexandra, who was still in Russia, he met fellow exile Natalia Sedova and married her shortly afterward. Interestingly, Trotsky took her last name, noting, "In order not to oblige my sons to change their name, I, for 'citizenship' requirements, took on the name of my wife." Trotsky and Sedova would have two sons, but like his two daughters from his first marriage, they would die before him.

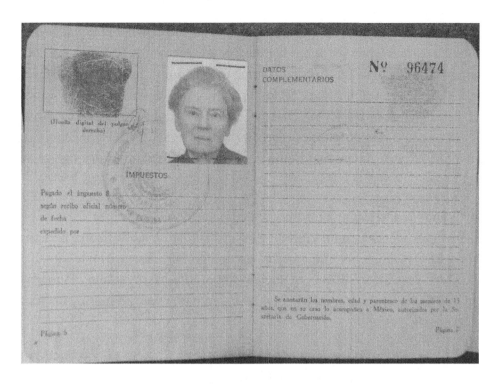

Natalia's passport

Despite the twists and turns of Trotsky's later life, Natalia would remain his companion until the end. Once again, though, Trotsky was only about two years into marriage when his domestic life was dramatically disrupted, this time by a surprising chain of events back in Russia. Quite suddenly, the discussions of revolution by the young men in London would cease to be mere theoretical debates.

With an incomplete education, Stalin had problems getting work. On the one hand, professional fields were not an option because he had no degree. On the other hand, he felt menial labor was beneath his dignity. Finally, he got a job tutoring children and, later, working as a clerk. These, however, were simply to allow him to eat. His true vocation lay in writing. He soon became a regular contributor to Brdzola Khma Vladimir, a socialist newspaper based out of Georgia.

Stalin made his first serious foray into politics in 1901, when he joined the Social Democratic Labor Party, whose main goal was to overthrow the Tsar through industrial organization and resistance. His activities within the party led to his first arrest in April of 1902, when he was sentenced to 18 months in prison for organizing a strike among the workers of a large factory in Batum, Georgia. Even after his stay in prison, however, his captors were still concerned that he was going to continue to be a problem, so they exiled him to the famed Russian frozen dessert, Siberia.

Not surprisingly, the determined Stalin didn't stay in Siberia long. Shortly after that Congress,

Stalin escaped in 1904 and quickly made his way back to Tiflis, where he once again began inciting workers to strike. Upon learning that the Social Democrats had split into two rival factions, Stalin naturally chose the Bolsheviks due to his admiration of Lenin. These activities brought him to the attention of his hero, Vladimir Lenin, who invited him to Tampere, Finland in late 1905 for a conference of Bolshevik leaders. Stalin was duly impressed by the massive gathering of workers and revolutionaries. He was also intrigued by the concept of democratic centralism, a mode of government that Lenin described as "freedom of discussion, unity of action."

    Completely committed to Lenin's teachings, Stalin spent the next eight years of his life promoting democratic centralism throughout Russia. Though his efforts got him arrested on four more occasions, he was never held long before escaping. One has to wonder at the ease with which he was able to thwart the efforts of such a supposedly harsh system. Perhaps his jailors were sympathetic to his cause or, more likely, their sympathy was bought by bribes from his fellow political rebels.

    It was also in the middle of the decade that Stalin met and married his first wife, Ekaterina "Kato" Svanidze, and they had their first child, a son, in 1907. When she died later that same year of typhus, Stalin lamented at her funeral, "This creature softened my heart of stone. She died and with her died my last warm feelings for humanity." His feelings for her would not stop him from killing several members of his first wife's family during the Great Purge, including her sister Mariko and brother Alexander.

Ekaterina

World War I

By the beginning of 1905, Russia was a veritable pressure cooker, exploding with political and social tensions in all sectors of society. In the major cities, industrial production had grown at a dizzying pace under the policies of Sergei Witte, Tsar Nicholas II's finance minister, creating a large dislocated urban underclass of precisely the sort that Marx had seen as the vanguard of revolution. The countryside was also teeming with discontent; when the serfs had been released from bondage, they had been given loans that were to finance the purchase of small holdings, a program that the tsarist government hoped would turn them into a large class of conservative property holders. But the generally small incomes Russian peasants were able to earn had left them crushed by mortgage payments they were often unable to make in full, and with little hope that they would be able to get out from under the debt they had incurred. Finally, the disastrous Russo-Japanese war left Russia broke and humiliated, creating widespread discontent among the populace.

In general, the government responded to expressions of protest with the kind of heavy-handed tactics that were applied to the young activists during the previous decade. This left very few confident that their grievances could be resolved through peaceful negotiation. The appeal of more radical approaches increased.

The Russian Revolution of 1905 began in a way that firebrands like Trotsky would have regarded as inauspicious. On Sunday, January 22, there was a peaceful march led by a Russian Orthodox priest, in which the protesters were carrying signs reading "Long Live the Tsar!" Inspired by the strikes that had overtaken a number of factories around St. Petersburg, the protesters intended to deliver to the Tsar himself a respectful petition of moderate demands for reform and dialogue. But upon arriving at the Winter Palace, the group was instructed by guards to turn back, and when it failed to do so, the guards began to fire indiscriminately into the crowd. A chaotic stampede followed, increasing the casualties.

Estimates of the number of deaths vary, but even the surely too conservative estimate of the Tsar's own regime counted 200 casualties, and most independently issued numbers are much higher. The massacre followed the pattern the revolutionaries knew all too well, where even peaceful voicing of dissent encountered a response so harsh that it allows for no dialogue, thus exacerbating the discontent into outright revolt. Such a radicalization is precisely what happened, on a countrywide scale, in the final week of January 1905.

The news of "Bloody Sunday" spread like wildfire across the Russian Empire, prompting massive strikes in its major cities, but the regime did not learn from its first mistake. More protesters were massacred in Riga and Warsaw within days of the initial slaughter in St. Petersburg. The strikes ultimately spread from factory workers to students and railway workers, leading to the forced paralysis of universities and railway lines. Ultimately and crucially, a series of mutinies began in the military, culminating in the famous mutiny of the *Battleship*

Potemkin in Trotsky's former home city of Odessa, later immortalized in Eisenstein's eponymous film.

Meanwhile, some of the remotest parts of the Empire were highly susceptible to the unrest, as local ethnic populations such as the Georgians, Armenians, Poles, Finns, and Baltic peoples had been seething for decades about the "Russification" policies that forced them to subordinate themselves culturally to Russia. Their demands for cultural autonomy and national self-determination mixed with the clamor for workers' rights and the economic grievances of the rural peasantry to create a state of fragmentation and chaos. When the Tsar's uncle, Grand Duke Sergei Alexandrovich, was assassinated by a bomb placed in his carriage, the Tsar finally decided to accept negotiation over reform. By late February, he accepted the principle of a broadened right to assembly and right of free speech, as well as reform measures to lessen the debt of the peasants and some form of popular political representation.

The Tsar's negotiations, mainly with elite liberal reformists, continued throughout the year as the country continued to explode with unrest among nearly every social group. In October of 1905, the Tsar reluctantly agreed to put his signature on a document that significantly expanded citizens' rights and created a clear path towards democratic governance, including universal suffrage. Although strikes and protests continued and were often met with brutal responses from the army and police, the October Manifesto, as it was called, gained widespread support because it seemed to leave the door open to further change by democratic means. There was also a large-scale amnesty of prisoners, which seemed to placate some of the popular rage.

However, the Russian people were exhausted by the end of 1905. The protests had led to thousands or even tens of thousands of deaths over the preceding year, as well as massive destruction of property and disruption of life. The populace had shown itself capable of bringing the entire country to a dead halt through synchronized strikes, but the Tsar's surprising willingness to compromise and open the door to reform had quelled tensions to some degree for the moment.

Naturally, the men in London were overjoyed by the events in 1905, especially because they viewed it as a fulfillment of their prophecy. Trotsky wrote:

> "The revolutionary masses are no more a theory, they are a fact. For the Social-Democratic Party there is nothing new in this fact. We had predicted it long ago. We had seen its coming at a time when the noisy liberal banquets seemed to form a striking contrast with the political silence of the people. The revolutionary masses are a fact, was our assertion. The clever liberals shrugged their shoulders in contempt. Those gentlemen think themselves sober realists solely because they are unable to grasp the consequences of great causes, because they make it their business to be humble servants of each ephemeral political fact. They think themselves sober statesmen in spite of the fact that history mocks at their wisdom, tearing to pieces

their schoolbooks, making to naught their designs, and magnificently laughing at their pompous predictions.

'There are no revolutionary people in Russia as yet' 'The Russian workingman is backward in culture, in self-respect, and (we refer primarily to the workingmen of Petersburg and Moscow) he is not yet prepared for organized social and political struggle.'…

Yes, the Revolution has begun. We had hoped for it, we had had no doubt about it. For long years, however, it had been to us a mere deduction from our "doctrine," which all nonentities of all political denominations had mocked at. They never believed in the revolutionary role of the proletariat, yet they believed in the power of Zemstvo petitions, in Witte, in "blocs" combining naughts with naughts, in Svyatopolk-Mirski, in a stick of dynamite ... There was no political superstition they did not believe in. Only the belief in the proletariat to them was a superstition,

History, however, does not question political oracles, and the revolutionary people do not need a passport from political eunuchs."

In a similar vein, Lenin wrote, "Only the most ignorant people can close their eyes to the bourgeois nature of the democratic revolution which is now taking place. Whoever wants to reach socialism by any other path than that of political democracy will inevitably arrive at conclusions that are absurd and reactionary both in the economic and the political sense."

Trotsky's role in the 1905 Revolution was both marginal and crucial. By the time Trotsky arrived in the country after the long journey from London, the strikes were already well underway, and many important political developments had occurred before he could make any impact on the trajectory of the revolution. He and the socialist leadership in London had had relatively little role in inciting any of the revolts; pus simply, a number of sectors of the population without a particularly confrontational political agenda had been radicalized by the events of Bloody Sunday and similar acts of unprovoked brutality on the part of the Tsarist government. That's not to say the 1905 Revolution ran counter to the basic Marxist theory of class struggle, since Marx and Engels believed the masses would be spontaneously led to revolt by the sheer exploitation and oppression to which they were being subjected. Whatever its general applicability, this was a fairly good description of what occurred in the Russian Empire in 1905. But the principal role of intellectuals like Trotsky in such a context, at least initially, was largely to catch up with events and determine the most advantageous role to be played in them. This is what he and his Menshevik and Bolshevik comrades tried to do.

Trotsky's role may also be regarded as crucial, however, because he continued to do his best to bridge the divide between Bolshevik and Menshevik, and in so doing, he became a leader with general appeal among the industrial workers then in revolt. While the theoretical differences between the two camps may have seemed all-consuming in their clandestine meetings in exile, in the heat of the struggles of 1905 they probably would have seemed petty and irrelevant to most of those actually involved in the strike. In the process of pursuing his "big tent" approach, Trotsky became one of the key figures in the St. Petersburg Soviet, which in turn made him an important part of what was probably the most important institutional development for the Russian workers movement during the revolutionary period. "Soviet" is a Russian word translatable to "council," but the St. Petersburg Soviet was the first open council of workers to gather and organize for workers' interests. It was created with some Menshevik involvement prior to Trotsky's appearance, but by dint of his charisma and rhetoric of unity he quickly rose to the position of vice chairman and then chairman by the end of 1905. When the Soviet was created, there had been no previous widely attended assembly intended to support the interests of the urban industrial workers, separate from the labor unions, which were regarded as highly compromised through government infiltration. Thus, from the perspective of radicals like Trotsky, the creation of the Soviet was a vital part of the process of making the proletarian revolution a reality.

In the meantime, the Russian imperial government and its elite liberal partners in dialogue were eager to do away with the more radical elements of the revolutionary sectors of society. For Trotsky and the other representatives of the Soviet, negotiation with the Tsar and piecemeal reform would have been nothing more than a ploy to squash the unstoppable momentum of the revolutionary movement that had been building throughout the year. Thus, to the radical revolutionaries, the October Manifesto was simply a reactionary sham that changed nothing about the basic necessity of revolt and resistance.

While the Tsarist government had loosened some of its restrictions on public speech critical of the Tsar and had opened the way to reforms that would have been unimaginable just a year earlier, after the October Manifesto the regime decided to clamp down on its more radical critics. The St. Petersburg Soviet was shuttered, and its leaders, including Trotsky, were arrested in late 1905 after refusing to recognize the authority of the government and announcing a new general strike to stop the piecemeal reforms. A new wave of repression, radiating out across the country, accompanied these arrests.

As the liberal reformist class negotiated with its new conservative interlocutors about the creation of a parliamentary monarchy, long-exiled Marxists like Trotsky found themselves in the same position they had been in at the turn of the century. They went from being political prisoners to being exiled. But if Trotsky had impressed the assembled workers of the Soviet with his speaking abilities, his blistering speech to the Tsarist court that brought him to trial in 1906 further consolidated his growing reputation for eloquence. He concluded his remarks to the court as follows:

"The prosecution invites us to admit that the Soviet armed the workers for the struggle against the existing 'form of government.' If I am categorically asked whether this was so, I shall answer: Yes! Yes, I am willing to accept this accusation. [But] let me ask: what does the prosecution mean by 'form of government'? Do we really have a form of government? For a long time past the government has not been supported by the nation but only by its military-police apparatus. What we have is not a national government but an automaton for mass murder. I can find no other name for the government machine which is tearing into parts the living body of our country. If you tell me that the pogroms, the murders, the burnings, the rapes . . . are the form of government of the Russian Empire – then I will agree with the prosecution that in October and November last we were arming ourselves, directly and immediately, against the form of government of the Russian Empire."

In retrospect, it is tempting to regard Trotsky as a prophet. Ultimately, the constitutional and parliamentary monarchy that was emerging out of the negotiations between Tsarists and liberals would fail, in large part because it was perceived by many as mere window dressing for the continued reactionary and repressive rule that preceded it and the brutal military apparatus that propped it up. But at the time, Trotsky's return to Siberian exile may have looked like a disastrous failure for what had been a workers' movement with unstoppable momentum. The 1905 Revolution certainly failed to bring about the desired effect that Lenin and other revolutionaries hoped it would, leading Lenin to believe that more forceful revolting was a necessity. A few years after the 1905 Revolution, Lenin would write:

"Notwithstanding all the differences in the aims and tasks of the Russian revolution, compared with the French revolution of 1871, the Russian proletariat had to resort to the same method of struggle as that first used by the Paris Commune — civil war. Mindful of the lessons of the Commune, it knew that the proletariat should not ignore peaceful methods of struggle — they serve its ordinary, day-to-day interests, they are necessary in periods of preparation for revolution — but it must never forget that in certain conditions the class struggle assumes the form of armed conflict and civil war; there are times when the interests of the proletariat call for ruthless extermination of its enemies in open armed clashes."

Though Lenin was back in Russia during these events, he showed little interest in the changes. Instead, he chose to bide his time and wait for the people to again despair of real hope within the current regime. In fact, he even encouraged his fellow Bolsheviks to take part in the Duma Elections of 1907, while he devoted his own time to raising money for future political activity.

It quickly becomes obvious that Lenin's fundraising methods went far beyond the modern concept of the thousand dollar a plate rubber chicken dinner. In addition to soliciting large donations from self-made Russian millionaires like Sava Morozov and Maxim Gorky, he also relied very heavily on donations raised through bank robberies successfully planned and executed by Bolshevik gangs. One such robbery, in which several people were killed, drew the ire of the Mensheviks, who began to distance themselves even further from Lenin and his followers.

It may have seemed at odds with Lenin's declaration at the Second Congress that violence and terror would not be accepted, but Lenin apparently had no scruples regarding how to finance his activities. Lenin converted most of the money into documents and utilized various papers and pamphlets he printed in an attempt to raise the political awareness of the general population of Russia. When that failed, he bribed leaders of the trade unions to influence their members toward socialism. He even went so far as to get one of his favorite men, Roman Malinovsky, elected to the head of the Metalworker's Union in St. Petersburg. This would prove to be a huge mistake.

Malinovsky

Forced by increasing scandal and suspicion to once again leave Russia, Lenin spent the next several months in seclusion. It was during this time that he created his most significant work, *Materialism and Empirio-criticism*. Published in secret in 1909, this book outlined the foundations for what is now referred to as Marxism-Leninism. In it he quotes everyone from philosophers and bishops to politicians and physicists in an attempt to prove that materialism is the root of all political evil. Writing at length about reason and nature, Lenin expounds upon philosophy, with quotes like, "The sole 'property' of matter with whose recognition philosophical materialism is bound up is the property of being an objective reality, of existing outside the mind."

Lenin left Russia again in 1911, this time moving to France to found the Bolshevik Party School to train political activists outside the prying eyes of the Russian police. He also devoted much of his time to meetings with his associates on how the Bolsheviks could take control of the Social Democratic Labor Party. However, when the 1912 annual meeting was held in Prague, he was unable to rally the votes in his favor. Instead, the Bolsheviks and Mensheviks split from each other completely and, from that day forward, maintained completely separate organizations. Such splinters didn't deter Lenin, who wholeheartedly supported removing those not fully committed to the same cause from the group. Around the time of the Second Congress, it was Lenin who noted, "Everyone is free to write and say whatever he likes, without any restrictions. But every voluntary association (including the party) is also free to expel members who use the name of the party to advocate anti-party views. Freedom of speech and the press must be complete. But then freedom of association must be complete too. I am bound to accord you, in the name of free speech, the full right to shout, lie and write to your heart's content. But you are bound to grant me, in the name of freedom of association, the right to enter into, or withdraw from, association with people advocating this or that view. The party is a voluntary association, which would inevitably break up, first ideologically and then physically, if it did not cleanse itself of people advocating anti-party views."

Though the revolutionary cause now had two disparate factions, Lenin did have one major success in Prague. He convinced the members to elect Malinovsky to the Bolshevik Central Committee, in spite of rumors that he was in fact a spy for the Okhrana, the Russian secret police. Lenin also convinced the party to run Malinovsky as a candidate for the Duma. They did, and he was elected in 1912, bringing the number of Bolsheviks in the Duma to six. Malinovsky soon distinguished himself among the group for his leadership and speaking abilities. Before giving any speech, however, he would send a copy to Lenin for his comments. What Lenin didn't know was that he was also sending a copy to the head of the Okhrana.

Armed with previews of speeches being made, as well as copies of letters exchanged between Lenin and Malinovsky, the Okhrana begin to make plans to split the Bolshevik party from within. When Malinovsky was instructed to set up a secret facility in Russia for printing subversive papers, the facility was quickly seized by the police and the people present arrested. Likewise, wherever Malinovsky travelled inside Russia to meet with fellow Bolsheviks, arrests soon followed.

Obviously all these "coincidences" fueled rumors that Malinovsky was indeed a spy.

However, Lenin remained unconvinced. In 1914, he wrote in Prosveshchenie:

"Martov and Dan have long been known and repeatedly exposed as slanderers. This has been spoken of dozens of times in the press abroad….And after this, Martov and Dan want us to agree to an investigation undertaken on their initiative, on the basis of their slanderous statements, and with the participation of the very groups that shield them! That is downright impudence, and sheer stupidity on the part of the slanderers. We do not believe a single word of Dan's and Martov's. We shall never agree to any "investigation" into insidious rumours with the participation of the liquidators and the groups that help them. This would mean covering up the crime committed by Martov and Dan. We shall however thoroughly expose it to the working class."

Lenin even threatened those who brought their concerns to his attention with banishment from the party. When he and Nadya moved to Austria in 1913 to organize a special meeting of twenty-two Bolshevik leaders, at least five of those attending were actually Okhrana spies. Thus, those two close allies, along with his own arrogance and ignorance, worked together to help keep one of his worst enemies as his best friend.

Lenin also had other interests of a more personal nature. Though some historians still dispute it, Lenin allegedly took a mistress, Inessa Armand, a married woman with four children. As usual, Lenin focused on what he wanted rather than what society told him was morally right. Armand was bright, musical and a politically ardent member of the Bolsheviks who hung on Lenin's every word. There were even rumors that they had a child together, though that remains unproven.

Armand

In keeping with their open minded views of marriage and morality, Lenin told Nadya all about his relationship with Armand, and if this bothered her, she never admitted it. In fact, in her autobiographical story, *Reminisces on Lenin*, she spoke kindly of Inessa, adding that life "became cozier and gayer when Inessa came. Our entire life was filled with party concerns and affairs, more like a student commune than like family life, and we were glad to have Inessa... Something warm radiated from her talk."

Meanwhile, 1911 found Stalin living in St. Petersburg, where he soon became the editor of the new magazine, Pravda ("truth"). By now, in closer conformance with the goals of the Bolsheviks, Stalin had mostly dropped his focus on Georgian independence and revolution, partly because the area was dominated by Mensheviks. Though he would always retain his thick Georgian accent, Stalin finally began writing predominantly in Russian.

For the next year, Stalin would be part of the weekly paper, published legally at that time. Still, the government always kept a close eye on their articles and censored anything they did not like. In order to try to avoid censorship, the staff constantly renamed the paper, giving it a total eight different title in two years.

Unfortunately for Stalin, one of his fellow editors, Miron Chernomazov, was actually an undercover agent with the Russian police. His reports to his superiors led to Stalin's arrest in March of 1913 and subsequent exile for life to Siberia. As a result, he was out of the country for the most pivotal events of Russian Communist history, the capture and execution of Nicholas II and his family. How much the tales of this blood-bathed coup influenced Stalin's future crimes against humanity is unclear. However, the event did set the tone for how Russian leadership would deal with enemies of the state for the rest of the 20th century.

Регистрационная карточка петербургского охранного отделения
с фотографическим снимком И. В. Сталина. (Фото)

A government card from a file used to keep tabs on Stalin

Just as he had after his first sentencing, Trotsky managed to flee from Siberia carrying false papers and travel clandestinely to London. The exile community around the Social Democratic party that had thrived prior to 1905 was now dispersed somewhat by the chaos of the preceding years, but the party's fifth congress was convened in the summer of that year.

At that congress, the division between Martov's Menshevik faction and Lenin's Bolsheviks continued to widen, and the congress was the scene of ferocious debates between the rival groups. Each side accused the other of heresy and betrayal of the party's revolutionary commitment, and though Trotsky continued to remain neutral in the conflict, the general perception was that he was closer to the Mensheviks in outlook and approach. That perception had been reinforced by his work with the St. Petersburg Soviet, which operated in far greater agreement with Menshevik principles of openness and loose organization than with the Bolshevik approach of clandestine activity and tightly centralized control.

Subsequent to the 1907 congress, Trotsky made his way to Vienna, a move that placed him in the center of much of the intellectual and cultural ferment of the early 20th century. His closest collaborator there was fellow Russian Adolph Joffe, with whom he founded the highly influential socialist newspaper *Pravda* ("Truth"), which they would publish until 1912. Throughout the Vienna years, the sniping between the Bolsheviks and Mensheviks continued, but *Pravda* became Trotsky's latest attempt to be a voice of "non-factional" socialist politics. Not long after the paper was shut down, Lenin and his allies began to publish another *Pravda*, which went on to become the official Communist Party organ in the Soviet Union. Throughout this period, the Bolsheviks attempted to woo Trotsky to their side, probably because of the influence and popularity he had achieved as leader of the Soviet and editor of *Pravda*, but he remained independent.

Trotsky with his daughter Nina in 1915

Perhaps because he was tired of living a double life, or maybe because of some desire for further adventure and fame, Malinovsky shocked Lenin and the other Bolsheviks by resigning from the Duma at the beginning of World War I and joining the Russian Army. He was wounded and captured the following year by the German Army and remained in a German Prisoner of War camp for the rest of the war. Still, Lenin forgave his old friend and continued to support him even as late as the end of 1916, when he reported that he felt sure Malinovsky regretted his rash move.

Malinovsky was hardly the only one who took to the fighting on behalf of his nation. Much to Lenin's chagrin, members of socialist parties across Europe rallied around their flags to support their countries, but Lenin felt that the war would be just one more example of poorer classes fighting the bourgeoisie's "imperialist war", instead of uniting together to engage in class warfare. In the year before the war broke out, Lenin asserted, "The bourgeoisie incites the workers of one nation against those of another in the endeavour to keep them disunited. Class-conscious workers, realising that the break-down of all the national barriers by capitalism is inevitable and progressive, are trying to help to enlighten and organise their fellow-workers from the backward countries."

When the war broke out, Lenin was living in Austria, one of the main belligerents of World War I and the one whose declaration of war on Serbia touched off the war after Archduke Franz Ferdinand was assassinated. After a brief detention by authorities, Lenin headed to neutral Switzerland. Now secure in a neutral country, Lenin could give full voice to his opinions on the Great War. In 1916, Lenin published one of his best known books, *Imperialism: The Highest Stage of Capitalism*. In the book, Lenin argued that imperialistic empire was the final stage of capitalism and the source of the current war. Even worse, to Lenin Russia's participation was serving nobody's interests but the French and British, making Russia the poorer class and its allies the bourgeoise. Instead of retaining this status quo, Lenin encouraged all the Allied troops, not just the Russians, to turn around and fire on their own officers instead of the Germans.

Though Lenin opposed the war, at least in the manner it was being fought between belligerent nations, he also understood the opportunity the war provided. While many were calling for the Russians to pull out of the war entirely, especially as Russian loses mounted, Lenin called instead for the people to "turn the imperialist war into a civil war." He wanted the people of Russia to use the opportunity of a distracted monarchy to rise up and overthrow the Romanovs.

Ironically, his push for continuing the war brought him into conflict with many of his fellow socialists, particularly Rosa Luxemburg. She was quick to point out that socialism or even democracy would not protect the Russian people from the Germans, but Lenin nevertheless maintained, "International unity of the workers is more important than the national." When the International Socialist Bureau Conference rolled around in Brussels in 1915, Lenin dispatched Inessa Armand to fight those who supported peace, including Luxemburg, Plekhanov, Trotsky and Martov. According to one historian, Lenin chose her instead of going himself because he trusted both her linguistic talent (she was fluent in five languages) and her loyalty to him.

Meanwhile, Trotsky left Zurich for Paris, but he was eventually deported by the French government, which was allied with Russia at the time and had no use for Russian revolutionaries. Trotsky was ultimately expelled from Europe altogether and put on an ocean liner heading to New York City.

Undeterred, Trotsky kept up his busy pace of activity on the other side of Atlantic, writing for radical newspapers and organizing Russian exiles, but he had not been in New York for three months before the news of revolution exploded once again out of Russia.

Revolution and Civil War

Lenin's plan for a Russian Civil War received a catalyst from a strange place. In September of 1915, Tsar Nicholas II dismissed his generals on the Eastern Front and took over military command himself. Thus, as the number of battles lost grew, his reputation and popularity among the people fell. By 1917, it was clear that the Russian Army would never be able to sustain further involvement in the war, having already lost almost 8 million soldiers to death, injury and capture. With that, the Russian people began to cry out against the privations of the war. Factory workers staged strikes for higher wages to pay the ever inflating cost of food for their families. At the same time, people in Petrograd rioted in the streets, vandalizing shops and demanding food that the government simply did not have.

Had he been wiser, Nicholas might have appealed to the people, or met with the Duma to work out some sort of solution to the shortages. However, he had been raised with the understanding that the main work of a Tsar was to preserve the monarchy for his son. Thus, he decided on the very inopportune moment of late February, 1917 to try to disband the Duma and regain absolute power. When the Duma refused to disband, the High Commander of the army appealed to Nicholas, suggesting that he should abdicate before a full scale revolution broke out. Some suggested that the Tsar's cousin, Grand Duke Michael Alexandrovich would make an excellent replacement. He refused, however, and on March 1, Nicholas was forced to leave and was replaced with a Provisional Government which originally consisted of a mishmash of parliamentary figures and members of revolutionary councils that had been elected by workers, soldiers and peasants.

Lenin was still in exile in Zurich when the February Revolution pushed Nicholas II out of power, and he only found out about it on March 15. Understandably thrilled with this turn of events, Lenin began firing off missives to friends and allies in an attempt to harness the revolutionary energy and direct it toward an international class conflict, writing in one letter, "Spread out! Rouse new sections! Awaken fresh initiative, form new organisations in every stratum and prove to them that peace can come only with the armed Soviet of Workers' Deputies in power." At the same time, he and other members of the Provisional Government went about trying to secure his safe passage back to Russia, and eventually a Swiss colleague with contacts in the German Foreign Ministry was able to get Lenin a train ride into Russia. While that seems odd at first glance, it is apparent the German Foreign Ministry hoped that Lenin's agitation back in Russia would sufficiently distract the Russian Army and lead to their surrender to Germany or their quitting of the war.

The locomotive that brought Lenin back to Russia

Joining Lenin on his private train were 27 fellow Bolsheviks anxious to press forward the cause of socialism and shape the new political system. Passing through Germany, some passengers on the train were "struck by the total absence of grown-up men. Only women, teenagers and children could be seen at the wayside stations, on the fields, and in the streets of the towns." Lenin, however, was all about business. While on the train, he completed work on what became known as his famous April Theses, and he read them aloud as soon as he entered Petrograd on April 3rd. In it he outlined his plans for the immediate future:

1.   In view of the undoubted honesty of the mass of rank and file representatives of revolutionary defencism who accept the war only as a necessity and not as a means of conquest,

in view of their being deceived by the bourgeoisie, it is necessary most thoroughly, persistently, patiently to explain to them their error, to explain the inseparable connection between capital and the imperialist war, to prove that without the overthrow of capital it is impossible to conclude the war with a really democratic, non-oppressive peace.

2.   The peculiarity of the present situation in Russia is that it represents a transition from the first stage of the revolution - which, because of the inadequate organization and insufficient class-consciousness of the proletariat, led to the assumption of power by the bourgeoisie - to its second stage which is to place power in the hands of the proletariat and the poorest strata of the peasantry.

3.   No support to the Provisional Government; exposure of the utter falsity of all its promises, particularly those relating to the renunciation of annexations. Unmasking, instead of admitting, the illusion-breeding "demand" that this government, a government of capitalist, should cease to be imperialistic.

4.   Recognition of the fact that in most of the Soviets of Workers' Deputies our party constitutes a minority, and a small one at that, in the face of the bloc of all the petty bourgeois opportunist elements who have yielded to the influence of the bourgeoisie.

It must be explained to the masses that the Soviet of Workers' Deputies is the only possible form of revolutionary government and that, therefore, our task is, while this government is submitting to the influence of the bourgeoisie, to present a patient, systematic, and persistent analysis of its errors and tactics, an analysis especially adapted to the practical needs of the masses.

5.   Not a parliamentary republic - a return to it from the Soviet of Workers' Deputies would be a step backward - but a republic of Soviets of Workers', Agricultural Labourers' and Peasants' Deputies throughout the land, from top to bottom.

Abolition of the police, the army, the bureaucracy. All officers to be elected and to be subject to recall at any time, their salaries not to exceed the average wage of a competent worker.

6.   In the agrarian program, the emphasis must be shifted to the Soviets of Agricultural Laborers' Deputies [including]

a.   Confiscation of private lands.

b.   Nationalization of all lands in the country, and management of such lands by local Soviets of Agricultural Labourers' and Peasants' Deputies.

c.   A separate organization of Soviets of Deputies of the poorest peasants.

d.   Creation of model agricultural establishments out of large estates.

7.   Immediate merger of all the banks in the country into one general national bank, over which the Soviet of Workers' Deputies should have control.

8.   Not the "introduction" of Socialism as an immediate task, but the immediate placing of the Soviet of Workers' Deputies in control of social production and distribution of goods.

9.   Party tasks [include] Immediate calling of a party convention and Changing the party program, mainly:

a.   Concerning imperialism and the imperialist war.

b.   Concerning our attitude toward the state, and our demand for a 'commune state."

c.   Amending our antiquated minimum program.

10.   Rebuilding the International. Taking the initiative in the creation of a revolutionary International, an International against the social-chauvinists and against the "center".

Although the turmoil had been limited to Russia so far, and the Theses were written about how to immediately create a socialist state in Russia, it's clear that Lenin envisioned an international revolution even at this early date. As one historian characterized his thinking in 1917, "Lenin made his revolution for the sake of Europe, not for the sake of Russia, and he expected Russia's preliminary revolution to be eclipsed when the international revolution took place. Lenin did not invent the iron curtain."

Lenin's April Theses were among the most radical writings of his life to date, and both Mensheviks and fellow Bolsheviks were taken aback. The Theses were roundly condemned by the Mensheviks (one of whom described them as the "ravings of a madman"), and initially the Theses were supported by only one prominent Bolshevik, Alexandra Kollontai.

Kollontai

One of the people that were concerned about Lenin's insistence on an immediate revolution was Stalin. While he had always been fascinated by Lenin's ideals, he was usually too pragmatic to begin a venture without an assurance of success. Stalin had been in exile himself until returning to Siberia, and by April he was the editor of the popular Bolshevik paper Pravda. Stalin could not remain silent forever. Though Stalin and other Bolsheviks still believed that the revolution should be a bourgeoise revolution, the Theses at least presented a party platform and a banner under which revolutionaries could rally and united. Thus, after wrestling with the issue for ten days, Stalin wrote a scathing article supporting Lenin and urging the peasants to rise up immediately. He further instructed them to begin by forming local committees that would confiscate large, privately owned estates and turn them over to the peasants that worked on them. Even still, Lenin was going in an ideologically different direction, one that brought him closer to the political leanings of Trotsky.

Trotsky's journey from New York to Russia was slowed by a last-ditch effort to keep him out of Russia by detaining him in Nova Scotia, but he arrived in May 1917. In the months that followed, he developed a closer relationships with the Bolsheviks, who at the time were a relatively weak and marginal player in the chaotic political scene. Soon after, he was arrested under orders from Kerensky, who distrusted him because of his fiery leadership of the Soviet and clear involvement in Bolshevik plots to seize power. However, Trotsky was not held long, and when he was released, his ferocious criticism of the Provisional Government was successful in swaying the urban workers and soldiers toward the Bolshevik position. He was about to become indispensable to Lenin.

The chaos continued when Alexander Kerensky, the new head of the Provisional Government, launched yet another military offensive against the Germans in July of 1917. Soldiers deserted by the thousands, with many of them carrying their government issued weapons back to the estates where they lived. They often used these guns to threaten or even kill their landlords so that they could have their land. They also burned stately mansions and moved ancient boundary stones to create new, smaller farms for the peasants themselves to own.

Kerensky

Alarmed by the rioting and believing that it was a result of the impact Lenin and other revolutionaries were having on the common people, Kerensky outlawed the Bolsheviks and tried to round up its members, outlandishly accusing them of being German agents. Trotsky famously defended Lenin and other Bolsheviks against the charge, exhorting, "An intolerable atmosphere has been created, in which you, as well as we, are choking. They are throwing dirty accusations at Lenin and Zinoviev. Lenin has fought thirty years for the revolution. I have fought [for] twenty years against the oppression of the people. And we cannot but cherish a hatred for German militarism . . . I have been sentenced by a German court to eight months' imprisonment for my struggle against German militarism. This everybody knows. Let nobody in this hall say that we are hirelings of Germany." Luckily for Lenin, he got wind of the threat well enough ahead of time to escape to Finland, where he completed work on *State and Revolution*, an outline of the government he hoped to one day see in Russia.

Lenin in disguise in Finland, 1917

As the rioting was going on back at home, Kerensky's July Offensive failed miserably, and he came into conflict with his new general, Lavr Kornilov, over policies related to discipline and production. When Kornilov sent the troops under his command to march on Kerensky's headquarters in Petrograd, Kerensky had to appeal to the Bolsheviks for Red Guards to protect his capitol city. Lenin reluctantly agreed and immediately recruited more than 25,000 soldiers to protect the government he so vehemently opposed. When Kornilov's troops saw the rows of dug in Red Guards, they refused to advance, and Kornilov surrendered to the palace police.

Realizing that he now had the Provisional Government largely at his mercy, Lenin returned to Russia in October and set up a party headquarters in Smolny Institute for Girls in St. Petersburg. From there, he quietly ordered that the Provisional Government be deposed and the Winter Palace vacated. On the evening of October 25, the Second All-Russian Congress of Soviets met at the Smolny Institute to establish a new government. While there were initially some disagreements over the overthrow of the Provisional Government, Martov's Mensheviks and Lenin's Bolsheviks eventually agreed to share power. Ironically, after all the drama that had surrounded the earlier months of that year, the October Revolution went largely unnoticed. As Lenin had written a month earlier, "The peaceful development of any revolution is, generally speaking, extremely rare and difficult ... but ... a peaceful development of the revolution is possible and probable if all power is transferred to the Soviets. The struggle of parties for power within the Soviets may proceed peacefully, if the Soviets are made fully democratic." It seemed that way in October.

Lenin arrived at the meeting the next evening to thunderous applause, appearing without a disguise for the first time since July. Famous American journalist John Reed, who would later chronicle the Russian Revolution in his critically acclaimed book, *Ten Days That Shook The World*, described Lenin for readers. "A short, stocky figure, with a big head set down in his shoulders, bald and bulging. Little eyes, a snubbish nose, wide, generous mouth, and heavy chin; clean-shaven now, but already beginning to bristle with the well-known beard of his past and future. Dressed in shabby clothes, his trousers much too long for him. Unimpressive, to be the idol of a mob, loved and revered as perhaps few leaders in history have been. A strange popular leader—a leader purely by virtue of intellect; colourless, humourless, uncompromising and detached, without picturesque idiosyncrasies—but with the power of explaining profound ideas in simple terms, of analysing a concrete situation. And combined with shrewdness, the greatest intellectual audacity."

Beginning his speech with "We shall now proceed to construct the Socialist order!", at the meeting, Lenin proposed a "Decree on Peace" calling for an end of the war, and a "Decree on Land" announcing that all property owned by large land owners and the aristocracy would be given to the peasants. Both decrees passed with little dissension. Next, the new government elected a Bolshevik majority to the Council of People's Commissars, with the Mensheviks joining the government a few weeks later. Lenin was soon elected Chairman of the Council, making him head of the government, though he had originally intended for the position to go to Trotsky, who declined because he worried his Jewish ethnicity would pose problems.

In recognition of his contribution, the now totally empowered Lenin appointed Stalin the Commissar of Nationalities, joking with him about his meteoric rise to power. As Commissar, Stalin was in charge of all the non-Russian people in the country, including Buriats, Byelorussians, Georgians, Tadzhiks, Ukrainians and Yakuts, nearly half the country's population. The spoiled little boy who'd been forced to speak Russian and had been teased about his appearance was now a bitter, angry man with nearly unlimited power. The combination would not make for a pretty outcome.

Initially, however, it looked like all would be well for these foreigners under Russian control. He concluded his famous Helsinki address of 1917 with these words of encouragement and promises of support:

"Comrades! Information has reached us that your country is experiencing approximately the same crisis of power as Russia experienced on the eve of the October Revolution. Information has reached us that attempts are being made to frighten you too with the bogey of famine, sabotage, and so on. Permit me to tell you on the basis of the practical experience of the revolutionary movement in Russia that these dangers, even if real, are by no means insuperable! These dangers can be overcome if you act resolutely and without faltering. In the midst of war and economic disruption, in the midst of the revolutionary movement which is flaring up in the West and of the increasing victories of the workers' revolution in Russia, there are no dangers or difficulties that could withstand your onslaught. In such a situation only one power, socialist power, can maintain itself and conquer. In such a situation only one kind of tactics can be effective, the tactics of Danton—audacity, audacity and again audacity! And if you should need our help, you will have it—we shall extend you a fraternal hand. Of this you may rest assured."

Unfortunately, the non-Russian peoples who heard or read this speech remained unconvinced. They were not so much interested in Russian help as they were national determination. Therefore they proved to be a constant source of stress to the new Commissar, setting up their own governments, opposing Bolshevik policy, and overall acting with the self-determination they had been promised, as long as they determined to join the new Union of Soviet Socialist Republics.

Faced with this level of opposition to his and the other Bolsheviks' plans, Stalin took a different tact. Accusing the new independent governments of being under the control of "the bourgeoisie," he agreed with Lenin that a more centralized government was needed. As the Russian Civil War played out during the early 1920s, Stalin became more involved in military matters while Lenin continued to focus on politics.

Trotsky, meanwhile, had become chairman of the Petrograd Soviet in St. Petersburg (which had its name changed to Petrograd during World War I to sound less German). Trotsky regained his reputation as a fiery and charismatic speaker with great sway over the city's working class. At the same time, during and after his prison stint, he solidified his relations with the Bolsheviks and Lenin and finally joined the party, ending his status as a factionless coalition-builder and severing his earlier ties to the Mensheviks, who had been allied with Kerensky's governing coalition.

Having seen how easily a multi-generational dynasty fell, Lenin was obviously concerned about keeping his own infant administration safe. To this end, he established "The Whole-Russian Extraordinary Commission for Combating Counter-Revolution and Sabotage" in the last weeks of 1917. Known colloquially as the Cheka (Extraordinary Commission), it soon became as feared by non-socialists as the Tsar's secret police had ever been. In addition to monitoring the movements of anyone opposing the government, the Cheka also enforced censorship laws against non-socialist newspapers.

Trotsky's immediate role after the revolution was Commissar of Foreign Affairs, and specifically his task was to negotiate the end of the devastating war with Germany, which had been a key Bolshevik promise throughout the war. Still, Trotsky had to walk a narrow line, particularly because he did not wish to provide aid or support to the reactionary Kaiser's government in Germany. In fact, Trotsky and the other Bolsheviks had long hoped that the German workers would be inspired by events in Russia and then rise up and spread the revolution across enemy lines.

While Lenin wanted Russia out of the war, he initially hoped to retain the land it had lost to the Germans. He worked with Trotsky to formulate a Russo-German treaty in which each country would agree to return any land gained from the other during the war. When this failed, he had to concede much of the Russian countryside to the Germans in return for pulling the Russians out of the war. The Treaty of Brest-Litovsk officially removed Russia from the conflict on March 3, 1918. However, it also resulted in Germany being so close to Petrograd that the government had to move its capital to Moscow.

Lenin and Fritz Platten

In spite of the Cheka's best efforts, those who opposed Lenin and the Bolsheviks were still out there, and they were gunning for Lenin, literally. In January 1918, gunmen shot at Lenin and Fritz Platten as they sat in an automobile after Lenin had given a speech, which Lenin survived after Platten pushed him down and shielded him. But the most famous assassination attempt would come in August 1918, when a supporter of the Socialist Revolutionary Party, Fanya Kaplan, approached Lenin as he sat in an automobile. After calling to him to get his attention, she fired at him three times, hitting him once in the arm and once in the jaw and neck. Though the wounds rendered him unconscious, Lenin survived the shooting, and fearful of people at the hospital who might try to finish the job, he returned to the Kremilin and ordered physicians to come there to treat him where he felt safe. Ultimately, doctors refused to perform surgery given the precarious position of the bullet in his neck. Pravda used the attempt for propaganda purposes, reporting, "Lenin, shot through twice, with pierced lungs spilling blood, refuses help and goes on his own. The next morning, still threatened with death, he reads papers, listens, learns, and observes to see that the engine of the locomotive that carries us towards global revolution has not stopped working..."

Fanya Kaplan

Despite that, Soviet officials began to downplay the attack, and many across Russia never learned of it. Though he survived the attack, the bullets were left in place and continued to erode his health. However, Lenin kept working and appearing in public, determined to keep the public ignorant of how weak his condition was becoming. This was important because Lenin was increasingly viewed as the embodiment of the new regime, and it was feared that his death could cause everything to crumble. One former Tsarist wrote as much, reporting after the attempt, "As it happens, the attempt to kill Lenin has made him much more popular than he was. One hears a great many people, who are far from having any sympathy with the Bolsheviks, saying that it would be an absolute disaster if Lenin had succumbed to his wounds, as it was first thought he would. And they are quite right, for, in the midst of all this chaos and confusion, he is the backbone of the new body politic, the main support on which everything rests.."

The Bolsheviks may have downplayed the assassination attempt publicly, but they were privately plotting retaliation on a massive scale. Two weeks before Kaplan's attempt on Lenin's life, the Petrograd Cheka chief Moisei Uritsky had been assassinated, and now Stalin suggested to Lenin that they should engage in "open and systematic mass terror…[against] those responsible." Thus, the Cheka, under the instruction of Stalin, launched what later came to be known as the "Red Terror" in response to the assassination attempt. In the weeks that followed, more than 800 people were executed, including the entire Romanov family. This however, was just the beginning. As the Bolsheviks, known popularly as the Red Russians fought an ongoing war against those who opposed socialism (the White Russians), more than 18,000 people were executed on charges related to opposing Lenin and his rule. While historians have often debated the extent of Lenin's personal involvement in the executions, Trotsky himself later asserted that it was Lenin who authorized the execution of the Russian Royal Family.

Though he is often remembered as a vocal opponent of Stalin's terror (and ultimately a victim of it), Trotsky was fully in support of the Cheka's methods and even took time to write and publish a full-throated defense of them in the book *Terrorism and Communism* (1920). He also defended the policies of "War Communism," including large-scale confiscation of produce, livestock, and grains in order to fuel the war effort, practices that placed a devastating burden on the rural poor in particular. Trotsky summed up his defense of all of these measures in *Terrorism and Communism*:

> "The more perfect the revolution, the greater are the masses it draws in; and the longer it is prolonged, the greater is the destruction it achieves in the apparatus of production, and the more terrible inroads does it make upon public resources. From this there follows merely the conclusion which did not require proof – that a civil war is harmful to economic life. But to lay this at the door of the Soviet economic system is like accusing a new-born human being of the birth-pangs of the mother who brought him into the world."

Victims of the Red Terror

Almost immediately after pulling Russia out of World War I, Trotsky found himself in charge of an equally daunting task: organizing the defense of the Bolshevik revolutionary state against the many enemies who had sprung up in succeeding months. These enemies, including Tsarists, liberals, and anti-Bolshevik leftists, all arrayed in violent and intractable opposition, often with significant foreign support. The Bolsheviks initially counted on a spontaneous campaign of support from the working classes, but the organizational weaknesses of their loyal force, the Red

Guard, soon displayed themselves. Trotsky was placed in charge of organizing the new Red Army that would defend the fragile revolutionary state against foes both native and foreign. Just after peace had been settled in Germany, it was time again to prepare for war.

Bolshevik propaganda depicting Trotsky as St. George slaying a dragon with the word counterrevolutionary on it.

Trotsky's placement at the helm of the Red Army was a surprising choice, given that he had no military experience and all of his battles up to that point had taken place in print, but if the Bolsheviks' enemies expected they would have little to fear from a force under the command of an intellectual with no training in war, they soon found themselves mistaken. Trotsky's overnight transformation into a brilliant martial tactician was perhaps paralleled in the 20th century only by that of fellow Marxist Che Guevara, who would go from asthmatic physician to effective guerrilla leader during the Cuban Revolution a generation later. To be fair, however, part of Trotsky's success in charge of the army resulted from his decision to recruit former Tsarist generals into leadership positions. This move was controversial among the Bolshevik leadership, which had little trust for anyone associated with the old regime, but Trotsky had recognized that the fierce commitment of Bolshevik recruits would be insufficient for the Red Army to stand its own against the many forces now assembled against it. The Tsarist officers were also recruited for their expertise and experience were monitored closely to ensure their continued loyalty by the newly created commissars, who enforced ideological purity.

Trotsky also instilled discipline in his forces through fear, which he believed was a necessary ingredient. In his autobiography, Trotsky asserted:

"An army cannot be built without reprisals. Masses of men cannot be led to death unless the army command has the death-penalty in its arsenal. So long as those malicious tailless apes that are so proud of their technical achievements—the animals that we call men—will build armies and wage wars, the command will always be obliged to place the soldiers between the possible death in the front and the inevitable one in the rear. And yet armies are not built on fear. The Tsar's army fell to pieces not because of any lack of reprisals. In his attempt to save it by restoring the death-penalty, Kerensky only finished it. Upon the ashes of the great war, the Bolsheviks created a new army. These facts demand no explanation for any one who has even the slightest knowledge of the language of history. The strongest cement in the new army was the ideas of the October revolution, and the train supplied the front with this cement."

At the same time, Trotsky still believed in the power of persuasion, and he sought to bring back deserters by appealing to their revolutionary instincts. He noted:

"In the provinces of Kaluga, Voronezh, and Ryazan, tens of thousands of young peasants had failed to answer the first recruiting summons by the Soviets … The war commissariat of Ryazan succeeded in gathering in some fifteen thousand of such deserters. While passing through Ryazan, I decided to take a look at them. Some of our men tried to dissuade me. 'Something might happen,' they warned me. But everything went off beautifully. The men were called out of their barracks. 'Comrade-deserters – come to the meeting. Comrade Trotsky has come to speak to you.' They ran out excited, boisterous, as curious as schoolboys. I had imagined them much worse, and they had imagined me as more terrible. In a few minutes, I was surrounded by a huge crowd of unbridled, utterly undisciplined, but not at all hostile men. The 'comrade-deserters' were looking at me with such curiosity that it seemed as if their eyes would pop out of their heads. I climbed on a table there in the yard, and spoke to them for about an hour and a half. It was a most responsive audience. I tried to raise them in their own eyes; concluding, I asked them to lift their hands in token of their loyalty to the revolution. The new ideas infected them before my very eyes. They were genuinely enthusiastic; they followed me to the automobile, devoured me with their eyes, not fearfully, as before, but rapturously, and shouted at the tops of their voices. They would hardly let me go. I learned afterward, with some pride, that one of the best ways to educate them was to remind them: 'What did you promise Comrade Trotsky?' Later on, regiments of Ryazan 'deserters' fought well at the fronts."

Trotsky reviewing soldiers in 1919

The forces of the so-called White Army, made up of anti-Bolshevik Russians of all stripes, and their allies from nearly all the major European nations, combined to place the new revolutionary regime in a state of siege. In response, the Bolsheviks introduced a number of policies that would set the stage for the state terrorism and suppression of later years.

White Army propaganda poster depicting Trotsky as Satan

   Unfortunately, bullets weren't all that was killing the Russian common people. While the Whites and Reds engaged in a civil war that would last for nearly 7 years, ordinary Russians were starving due to war time communism measures that allowed the Soviet government to confiscate food for soldiers from peasant farms with little or no payment. When the farmers retaliated by growing fewer crops, the Cheka responded by executing or imprisoning the offending peasants. However, even the Cheka could not cause plants to grow, and during the Famine of 1921, more than 5 million Russians starved to death in and near their own homes. This tragedy, along with the civil unrest it provoked, led Lenin to institute the New Economic Policy to rejuvenate the both agriculture and industry.

In formulating his economic policies, Lenin asserted, "We must show the peasants that the organisation of industry on the basis of modern, advanced technology, on electrification, which will provide a link between town and country, will put an end to the division between town and country, will make it possible to raise the level of culture in the countryside and to overcome, even in the most remote corners of land, backwardness, ignorance, poverty, disease, and barbarism." Of course, to Lenin that meant total State control over industry, and he implemented a system in which every industry was overseen by one ruling official granted all the deciding power over any disputes, thereby completely curbing workers' self-management rights.

Тов. Ленин ОЧИЩАЕТ землю от нечисти.

A propagandist picture that reads, "Comrade Lenin Cleanses the Earth of Filth"

Lenin's first non-political interest was in bringing electricity to all of Russia, so that the homes and factories could be modernized. Disappointed with the lack of progress made by factories under their own power, Lenin made the first of many moves to expand government control over private lives by placing businesses under the supervision of Soviet committees. These committees would evaluate everything from worker rights to productivity to the flow of materials. They would then report to the government, who would, it was hoped, take steps to help the factories improve their productivity.

Having established a plan for economic improvements, Lenin turned his attention to social issues. First, he instituted a system of free health care for all Russians, as well as a widespread system of public education. With the encouragement of both his wife and his mistress, he encouraged the government to grant women the right to vote, and to encourage them to take advantage of higher education to train to enter the work force.

Like Trotsky, Stalin also cut his teeth in the Russian Civil War, and his military strategy was as effective as it was ruthless. Prior to his successful battle against the White Army at Tsaritsyn, he met with the local leaders on a boat tied up along the shore of the Volga River. It is rumored that he interviewed them thoroughly and then sent the ones he believed to be loyal back to their homes and offices. The ones whose loyalty he questioned were summarily shot and thrown in the river.

Stalin's desire for blood had been fed by the assassination of Moisei Uritsky and the attempt on the life of Lenin himself in August, 1918. In a telegram to the badly wounded Lenin on August 31, Stalin committed himself to revenge:

"Having learned of the villainous attempt of the hirelings of the bourgeoisie on the life of Comrade Lenin, the world's greatest revolutionary and the tried and tested leader and teacher of the proletariat, the Military Council of the North Caucasian Military Area is answering this vile attempt at assassination by instituting open and systematic mass terror against the bourgeoisie and its agents."

Lenin passed Stalin's recommendation on to Felix Dzerzhinsky, the head of Soviet state security, who in turn instituted the famous Red Terror the next day. The unintended consequence of this genocide was that the Bolsheviks government became increasingly unpopular with the common Russian people. While they supported the ideas of freedom and brotherhood in general, they were not terribly sanguine about seeing more and more people around them hauled from their homes and shot. Many could sense the mania in the air and they wanted no part of it.

Following the Kronstadt Uprising in which Soviet military men and civilians teamed up to call for an end to the random slaughter of their countrymen, Lenin loosened up the government's control on economic policy. He even instituted the New Economic Policy, which allowed farmers to once again sell their produce in local markets. Those who needed to could even employ others to work for them without falling under the suspicion of being wealthy landowners. Those who did not farm were also allowed more freedom to own and run private businesses, including small factories.

While Stalin agreed with the New Economic Policy, others did not, and fighting to keep it alive began to take its toll of Lenin's health. Thus, in April of 1922, he met with other party leaders and asked that Stalin be appointed the first General Secretary of the Soviet Union. One of Stalin's powers as General Secretary allowed him to dismiss any party members he deemed useless or disloyal. Coincidentally, he quickly discovered the most of the followers of his arch rival, Leon Trotsky, fell into this category. Therefore, he was able to remove from party participation thousands of otherwise loyal members. He replaced them with members whom he knew to be loyal to him, and whose continued loyalty he could count on, since their comfortable positions depended on it.

No one thought much of this move since Lenin appeared to still be in complete charge of the party, and it passed with little discussion. However, when Lenin suffered a stroke a few months later and was left paralyzed, either Trotsky or Stalin seemed to be the next in line.

Stalin's Rise to Power

Throughout all this time, Lenin remained in increasingly poor health due to the bullets still in his body, as well as the fact that he was working upwards of 14-16 hours per day running the new nation. Russian historian Dmitri Volkogonov famously described a typical work day for the premier: "Lenin was involved in the challenges of delivering fuel into Ivanovo-Vosnesensk... the provision of clothing for miners, he was solving the question of dynamo construction, drafted dozens of routine documents, orders, trade agreements, was engaged in the allocation of rations, edited books and pamphlets at the request of his comrades, held hearings on the applications of peat, assisted in improving the workings at the "Novii Lessner" factory, clarified in correspondence with the engineer P. A. Kozmin the feasibility of using wind turbines for the electrification of villages... all the while serving as an adviser to party functionaries almost continuously."

Lenin working in the Kremlin, 1918

In April of 1922, doctors finally decided to remove the bullet in Lenin's neck, but after a month spent resting and recovering, Lenin returned to his grueling schedule. This proved to be too much for his fragile physical state and he suffered a stroke just a month later. Though it affected his speech and his movement on the right side, he began to gradually recover by June and made the imprudent choice of going back to work. In addition to resuming duties in August, he also delivered a series of long speeches in November.

Lenin and Stalin after Lenin's first stroke

Even as Trotsky's Red Army was successfully beating back the advances of the White Army, he was becoming embroiled in the conflicts that would ultimately bring about his political demise. By 1921, it was clear that Lenin's health was deteriorating rapidly, and those in the inner circles of the Bolshevik leadership began to contemplate their leader's succession. Trotsky was at once Lenin's most visible ally and therefore his most likely successor, but he was an object of suspicion among other members of the Bolshevik Central Committee because he had not joined the party until the middle of 1917. Conversely, most of the others had stood with Lenin's faction from the beginning of the split with the Mensheviks, including Stalin, a less publicly known but increasingly significant player with whom Trotsky sparred over tactical issues throughout the Civil War period and after.

After the first stroke, weakened by his physical condition, Lenin fell prey to Stalin's ambition. In October of 1922, the Central Committee voted to accept Stalin's foreign trade policy instead of the one put forward by Lenin. Seeing the handwriting on the wall, Lenin contacted Trotsky and suggested that they team up to try to hold Stalin in check. Trotsky agreed, and together they saw Stalin's policy overturned at the next committee meeting.

Unfortunately for Lenin, he had employed Stalin's wife, Nadya, as his secretary. She found a copy of the letter he sent to Trotsky and shared its contents with her husband. He in turn called Lenin's wife, Nadezhda, and berated her over the phone for allowing her weak and obviously delusional husband to write such a letter. This phone call sealed Stalin's fate in Lenin's eyes, and he dictated a letter in which he suggested that Stalin was not fit to take his place as the party's leader.

Sensing death was coming after the first stroke, Lenin began dictating instructions on how he would like the Soviet government to be continued, comprising what came to be known as Lenin's Testament near the end of 1922. In addition to dictating how the Soviet government should be structured, it was particularly notable in its criticism of several high-ranking officials, including Stalin, Trotsky, Grigory Zinoviev, Lev Kamenev, and Nikolai Bukharin. Lenin was extremely concerned about Stalin, who had become Communist Party's General Secretary in 1922. In it he compared Stalin negatively to Trotsky, saying,

"Comrade Stalin, having become General Secretary, has concentrated an enormous power in his hands; and I am not sure that he always knows how to use that power with sufficient caution. On the other hand, Comrade Trotsky, as was proved by his struggle against the Central Committee in connection with the question of the People's Commissariat of Ways and Communications, is distinguished not only by his exceptional abilities – personally he is, to be sure, the most able man in the present Central Committee – but also by his too far-reaching self-confidence and a disposition to be too much attracted by the purely administrative side of affairs."

Lenin completed this letter on Christmas Day, 1922. However, a few days later, perhaps concerned that he had not made his concerns sufficiently clear, he added the following post-script.

"Stalin is too rude, and this fault, entirely supportable in relations among us Communists, becomes insupportable in the office of General Secretary. Therefore, I propose to the comrades to find a way to remove Stalin from that position and appoint to it another man who in all respects differs from Stalin only in superiority – namely, more patient, more loyal, more polite and more attentive to comrades, less capricious, etc. This circumstance may seem an insignificant trifle, but I think that from the point of view of preventing a split and from the point of view of the relation between Stalin and Trotsky which I discussed above, it is not a trifle, or it is such a trifle as may acquire a decisive significance."

Lenin simply burned his body out by continuing to push it to its physical limits, and he suffered a second stroke in December of that same year, which partly paralyzed the right side of his body. The third and final stroke in March of 1923 proved his final undoing, rendering him mute and bedridden.

Lenin after his third stroke

Site of Lenin's death

On January 21, 1924, Lenin's body finally gave out, and he died that night in his estate at Gorki at just 53 years old. For four days his body lay in state, during which time nearly a million mourners passed through to see it. By then, Petrograd had been renamed Leningrad. Most famously, Lenin's body was embalmed and placed for public display in Lenin's Mausoleum, where plenty of visitors can still pass by his body and view it each day. It is estimated that over 100 million have viewed his body in the last 88 years.

Pallbearers carrying Lenin's coffin

Throughout the period of Lenin's illness and the successful winding down of the Civil War, the issues that had divided the Mensheviks and the Bolsheviks two decades before reemerged as subjects of practical debate. First of all, there was an economic debate about whether the confiscatory policies of "War Communism" should continue. The Bolsheviks had to decide whether to move the country rapidly toward a communistic model of production as envisioned by Marx, or whether there should be a loosening of restrictions on economic activity in order to foster and incentivize a resurgence of production after many harsh years of war. The latter proposal proceeded from the old assumption that the under-industrialized Soviet economy was not yet ready for the transition to full-scale socialism, and therefore needed to undergo further capitalistic development with this ultimate goal in mind. In part because of the strikes and uprisings provoked by the harsh regime of "War Communism," the Bolshevik leadership ultimately acceded to this more liberalized regime, dubbed the "New Economic Policy."

A second question reprised in these years was the question of how centralized the party, and therefore the state, should be. Should trade unions and other workers' organizations be able to obtain some autonomy? Trotsky, who took charge of rebuilding the national railways after the end of the Civil War, initially argued against trade union autonomy, but soon after that he came to criticize the increasing concentration of power among the party's inner circle. Of course, that concentration of power was being led by Stalin in his capacity as General Secretary of the party, and it was accepted by his allies Kamenev and Zinoviev.

The factional struggles of the Bolsheviks in the 1920's make for a convoluted story, but they can be understood as ideological struggles over how to implement communism and personal struggles between highly ambitious men. The splits within the party continued the fundamental questions about party organization that divided the Bolsheviks from their opponents in the first place. Stalin and his allies opted for a model of highly concentrated and centralized power wielded by a small revolutionary vanguard, while Trotsky and the so-called Left Opposition advocated a greater openness and pluralism advanced through the democratic institution of the Soviets. This is not to say that Trotsky took a more tolerant view of opposition to the Bolshevik agenda; he had personally advocated the persecution of Mensheviks, Social Revolutionaries, and other rivals on the left, consigning them in one famous speech to the "dustbin of history." But the more Trotsky saw of the concentration of power in the hands of a new governing elite, the more wary he became.

At the same time, the ideological affiliations of both Trotsky and Stalin in this period seem to have been partially strategic. Each assumed their respective positions at least in part to attempt to position themselves against the other in what was emerging as an epic battle of will. Trotsky recognized the battle lines being drawn as early as 1919, noting, "It is no wonder that my military work created so many enemies for me. I did not look to the side, I elbowed away those who interfered with military success, or in the haste of the work trod on the toes of the unheeding and was too busy even to apologize. Some people remember such things. The dissatisfied and those whose feelings had been hurt found their way to Stalin or Zinoviev, for these two also nourished hurts."

Lenin was the unquestioned head of the new Soviet Union, and upon his death he had firmly expressed the desire to make sure Stalin didn't concentrate power and control over the young Communist nation. Of course, that's precisely what ended up happening. So how and why did Lenin's Testament go unheeded?

Trotsky was in the faraway Caucasus when Lenin finally died in the beginning of 1924, and he reacted by writing, "And now Vladimir Ilyich is no more. The party is orphaned. The workmen's class is orphaned. This was the very feeling aroused by the news of the death of our teacher and leader." But Stalin and his allies took advantage of their rival's absence to suppress documents written by Lenin shortly before his death that pleaded for the reconciliation of the factions. They also used the absence of Trotsky from the leader's funeral as an opportunity to resurrect insinuations about his loyalty.

When Lenin's widow unearthed the document for Soviet officials, it was quickly disregarded and suppressed by Stalin, Kamenev, and Zinoviev, the ruling troika that Lenin had disparaged. Other leaders also went about making sure the Testament had no effect, including Trotsky, who published an article countering its importance and asserting that they were not a will and had not technically been violated. It was a stance Trotsky himself would come to regret in ensuing years as his opposition to Stalin increased.

While the letter made clear Lenin's intentions, it did not have the force of law behind it, especially with the remaining Soviet leaders asserting that it was not a final will. Since Lenin died before he could use his own personal leadership to enforce his wishes, Stalin became the preeminent Soviet leader. At the same time, his battle with Lenin had given him a sense of the bigger picture, and he now saw the wisdom of moving more slowly, especially when dealing with the common people. Therefore, he initially left the New Economic Policy in place and even allowed the farmers to buy up land around them to expand their farms. These larger landowners were known at kulaks, meaning "fists" for the tight way in which they held on to their land.

On the political front, Stalin had other things on his mind. As the General Secretary of the Soviet Union, he courted the favor of Lev Kamenev and Grigory Zinoviev, two powerful members of the Politburo, to keep Trotsky in check. He encouraged rumors that Trotsky would probably oust them if he came to power so that he could put his own people in power. He also encouraged a sense of his superiority, along with theirs, against the upstart Trotsky, who hadn't even joined the party until 1917.

Kamenev

Zinoviev

Trotsky initially thought he had an ace in the hole: Lenin's last letter. In 1924, he persuaded Lenin's widow to demand its publication. However, Zinoviev was one step ahead of him and made an impassioned speech indicating that the great leader's fears had been unfounded, since the party had prospered so well under Stalin's leadership. Since a majority of the members of the Central Committee had been appointed by Stalin himself, they quickly agreed that Zinoviev was right and the letter remained unpublished.

Heady with the success of once again standing down his old enemy, Stalin moved in for the kill. In 1925, he worked with his allies on the Central Committee to have Trotsky removed from office. Though his supporters urged him to fight the decision, with arms if necessary, Trotsky had had enough of politics and agreed to resign quietly.

As soon as he no longer needed their help against Trotsky, Stalin began to speak openly against Kamenev and Zinoviev. He attacked Trotsky's position that the role of the Soviet Union should be to spread communism throughout the world, a position also held by Zinoviev and Kamenev. Instead, he maintained that it was more important to solidify and maintain power within the states of the Soviet Union. This put Kamenev and Zinoviev in an awkward position, since they didn't want to oppose a powerful ally and come to agree with a man they had just helped depose.

Since Zinoviev and Kamenev seemed unlikely to continue to support Trotsky, Stalin felt secure enough to turn his political attention to other members of the Central Committee. However, the men soon overcame their embarrassment about their past attacks on Trotsky and finally publically joined forces with him against Stalin in 1926. By that time, however, it was too late. Stalin, accusing them of promoting disharmony and disunity, had them thrown off the Central Committee. Since a political split into a two party system was among the Soviet Union's greatest fears, Zinoviev and Kamenev agreed to resign quietly. Trotsky, on the other hand, made no such promises and was banished to Kazakhstan.

Ironically, when Trotsky was expelled from a Communist Party now thoroughly dominated by Stalin in 1927, his old enemy Zinoviev was expelled alongside him. Now disempowered but still enjoying popular support, Trotsky was far too dangerous for Stalin to allow to remain in the country. He was sent into exile for the third and final time through Russia's southwestern border with Turkey.

Trotsky's home in Istanbul, Turkey

With his political position secured, Stalin turned his attention toward his country's economic situation. In order to make the farms across the Soviet Union produce enough food to feed the ever expanding population, Stalin learned that the farmers would need 250,000 new, gas powered tractors. Not only did these need to be built, but they would need to be powered, so he also had to find a way to pump and refine the extensive oil deposits lying underground in much of the northern regions of the country. Finally, farms needed electricity, which meant more power plants and wires strung across great distances.

In order to accomplish this, Stalin had to get more factories up and running. They had just barely gotten back to their pre-Revolution level of production, much less seen any growth. However, he was determined, and brought the same force that he had already used against the Politburo to bear on the factories. To this end, he created and enforced in 1928 the first of many Five Year Plans.

He began by going after the kulaks. They tended to grow and sell food near their own homes and villages, while he wanted more produce imported into the cities to feed the factory workers and their families. Therefore, in 1928 he began pressuring them to abandon their independent farms and join together as collectives.

Not surprisingly, Stalin's promises of higher production and better profits largely fell on deaf ears. Though he tried to explain that, as part of a cooperative, the farmers could pool their resources and buy better equipment, the men and women who had worked the same land for generations were less than enthusiastic. This did not please Stalin at all, and perhaps even stirred up memories of the peasants who had teased him as a young boy. They definitely stood for all that he had tried to put behind him when he left Gori for the big city.

Frustration often brings out the worst in people, and this was so for Stalin. He ordered his underlings on the local level to take possession of the kulak's land and have them gathered together into state owned collective farms. Those who resisted were shot out right, including thousands of kulak farmers and their families. Furthermore, anyone else who got in his way was sent to Siberia or Russian holdings in Central Asia. According to Soviet records, about 1 in 4 failed to survive the trip.

At the same time Stalin was also determined to see growth in factory output. He set goals for tremendous increases in the production of coal, iron and electricity. He spread rumors that, if these goals were not met, the Soviet Union would be in danger of eminent invasion. He also encouraged factory managers to set high goals for their workers and to publically ostracize those that did not meet them.

Discouraged by insurmountable demands, many workers simply stopped coming in for work. If this became a pattern for an individual, he would be arrested and charged with sabotage by not working hard enough to support the Five Year Plan. If deemed guilty, the worker could be sent to a forced labor camp, either on the dreaded Siberian Railway or along the Baltic Sea Canal. The worst offenders were shot outright as a warning to others.

To be fair, Stalin did not only authorize threats and punishments to motivate workers. He also pushed the Central Committee to offer higher wages to those who excelled. Committee members argued against what they saw as a betrayal of the egalitarian principles of the revolution, but in the end Stalin prevailed, and by the early 1930s those who developed the necessary skills to serve the good of the people could expect to be rewarded with higher wages.

Though his he had won the battle for higher wages, Stalin was in grave danger of losing the war over control of the Politburo. By the summer of 1932, opposition to his policies had risen to such a fevered pitch that members were calling for his expulsion and the reinstatement of Leon Trotsky to power. Not surprisingly, Stalin met this threat aggressively and demanded that those who dared criticize him should be rounded up and shot. At this, even one his staunchest supporters, Sergei Kirov, argued that he had gone too far, and the plan was never executed.

Kirov

By the end of 1932, first Five Year Plan had come to an end and it was time to evaluate its success. In a report to the Politburo, Stalin described the results:

1.   The results of the five-year plan have refuted the assertion of the bourgeois and Social-Democratic leaders that the five-year plan was a fantasy, delirium, an unrealizable dream. The results of the five-year plan show that the five-year plan has already been fulfilled.

2.   The results of the five-year plan have shattered the well-known bourgeois "article of faith" that the working class is incapable of building the new, that it is capable only of destroying the old. The results of the five-year plan have shown that the working class is just as well able to build the new as to destroy the old.

3.   The results of the five-year plan have shattered the thesis of the Social-Democrats that it is impossible to build socialism in one country taken separately. The results of the five-year plan have shown that it is quite possible to build a socialist society in one country; for the economic foundations of such a society have already been laid in the U.S.S.R.

4.   The results of the five-year plan have refuted the assertion of bourgeois economists that the capitalist system of economy is the best of all systems, that every other system of economy is unstable and incapable of standing the test of the difficulties of economic development. The results of the five-year plan have shown that the capitalist system of economy is bankrupt and unstable; that it has outlived its day and must give way to another, a higher, Soviet, socialist system of economy; that the only system of economy that has no fear of crises and is able to overcome the difficulties which capitalism cannot solve, is the Soviet system of economy.

5.   Finally, the results of the five-year plan have shown that the Communist Party is invincible, if it knows its goal, and if it is not afraid of difficulties.

Of course, Stalin's report failed to mention that despite his collectivization and modernization, famines across the Soviet Union resulted in the deaths of upwards of 5-10 million people. Stalin has been blamed for engineering the Ukrainian famine, to the extent that he has been accused of genocide for the mass starvation.

Hoping to smooth over relations between Stalin and the rest of the party, Kirov suggested in 1934 that Stalin allow those who'd been exiled for opposing him to return home. Stalin did not like this idea, and spent much of that summer trying to persuade Kirov to come back to his way of thinking. Kirov would not agree, however, and was assassinated on December 1 of that year.

Stalin claimed to know nothing of any assassination plot and insisted instead that it was the work of Trotsky and his followers. He had 17 suspects arrested, convicted and executed, including former colleagues Grigory Zinoviev and Lev Kamenev. This was just the beginning, however, and in the years that followed Stalin continued to cleanse the party of those who opposed him. With the help of Nikolai Yezhov, whom he made head of the Communist Secret Police, he saw one member after another arrested, interrogated until they confessed, and executed. By 1938, Stalin had purged so many veteran officials that he felt secure enough to stop the purges, and Yezhov became the fall guy for the excesses of the Great Purge. As a result, Yezhov was forced from his position, and his knowledge of Stalin's Great Purge made him too much of a risk to even try in public, so Yezhov was secretly executed and disposed of in 1940. After his death, Yezhov was very memorably removed from a photo showing him and Stalin, one of the most famous examples of the Soviets' historical revision.

Yezhov

   Having purged the government of his enemies, Stalin turned his attention to the Soviet Army.
While some historians have argued that Stalin's severe attacks on his fellow countrymen were
motivated by nothing more than a paranoid need to solidify power, others maintain that he did
indeed have cause for concern. Rumors definitely abounded of coups and attempted coups in the
works. However, whether there was any truth behind those rumors remains a mystery.

   Whatever his motivation, Stalin showed his usual thorough ruthlessness. In June of 1937 he
had eight of his top commanders arrested and charged with conspiracy with Nazi Germany
against the Soviet Union. The men were convicted and summarily executed. But this was just
the beginning. For the next few years, the Red Army was indeed red, with the blood of 30,000
executed soldiers, including half of all the commissioned officers.

   With the government and army thoroughly cleansed of opposition, Stalin attacked the

Communist Secret Police. He appointed a new head, Lavrenti Beria, whom he charged with ferreting out what he called "fascist elements" that he claimed had infiltrated the police force. In reality, it was Baria's job to round up those who knew the details behind the recent killing spree and to see to it that they were silenced. In doing this, he had every leader of the police force executed.

   Trotsky remained for four years in Turkey, followed by periods living in France, Norway, and finally Mexico, where he remained until his death in 1940. He continued to write at a furious pace throughout this period, composing his own history of the 1917 Revolution and a detailed analysis of what he regarded as the perversion of socialism by Stalin's bureaucracy, which he expounded on in greatest detail in his book *The Revolution Betrayed* (1936). At the same time, he organized an international movement of communists opposed to what was now called "Stalinism", a project that culminated in the creation of the Fourth International as an alternative to the Third International, the global communist organization now controlled by the Soviet state.

Trotsky reading the *Militant* in exile

   Trotsky was a vocal and tireless critic of Stalin's grotesque "show trials," the humiliating convictions of Bolshevik leaders for alleged counter-revolutionary subversion. In the foreword of *The Stalin School of Falsification*, Trotsky wrote, "THE MOSCOW TRIALS, which so shocked the world, signify the death agony of Stalinism. A political regime constrained to use such methods is doomed. Depending upon external and internal circumstances, this agony may endure for a longer or shorter period of time. But no power in the world can any longer save Stalin and his system. The Soviet regime will either rid itself of the bureaucratic shell or be sucked into the abyss."

It was through this criticism that Trotsky gained his reputation as an advocate of a humane and democratic socialism. Trotsky's earlier writings about the use of Red Terror make that reputation problematic at best and disingenuous and flatly wrong at worst, but Trotskyist organizations did ultimately become an incubator of dissenting, non-doctrinaire leftist movements.

In 1937, Trotsky crossed the Atlantic to Mexico, where he took advantage of the welcome offered by a progressive but non-communist government. He mingled with the communist-leaning intelligentsia of Mexico City, including a stint living in the home of the painters Diego Rivera and Frida Kahlo. He also received visits from allies and sympathizers around the globe and organized with the emerging Socialist Workers' Party in the United States.

But even though he was exiled half a world away, Trotsky's days were numbered. Stalin feared his rival's growing international status, and he was never squeamish about the need for extreme methods to silence a potential enemy. Trotsky himself seemed prepared for the possibility, penning what is now called his testament in February 1940:

> "In addition to the happiness of being a fighter for the cause of socialism, fate gave me the happiness of being her husband. During the almost forty years of our life together she remained an inexhaustible source of love, magnanimity, and tenderness. She underwent great sufferings, especially in the last period of our lives. But I find some comfort in the fact that she also knew days of happiness.
>
> For forty-three years of my conscious life I have remained a revolutionist; for forty-two of them I have fought under the banner of Marxism. If I had to begin all over again I would of course try to avoid this or that mistake, but the main course of my life would remain unchanged. I shall die a proletarian revolutionist, a Marxist, a dialectical materialist, and, consequently, an irreconcilable atheist. My faith in the communist future of mankind is not less ardent, indeed it is firmer today, than it was in the days of my youth.
>
> Natasha has just come up to the window from the courtyard and opened it wider so that the air may enter more freely into my room. I can see the bright green strip of grass beneath the wall, and the clear blue sky above the wall, and sunlight everywhere. Life is beautiful. Let the future generations cleanse it of all evil, oppression and violence, and enjoy it to the full.
>
> L. Trotsky
>
> 27 February 1940

Coyoacan"

In May 1940, a cadre of Spanish and Mexican communists loyal to Stalin, including the important Mexican painter David Alfaro Siqueiros, assaulted Trotsky's home in an attempted hit. Trotsky survived, but he knew this would not be the last attempt against him. He published an account of the attempted hit, describing it vividly:

"The attack came at dawn, about 4 A. M. I was fast asleep, having taken a sleeping drug after a hard day's work. Awakened by the rattle of gun fire but feeling very hazy, I first imagined that a national holiday was being celebrated with fireworks outside our walls. But the explosions were too close, right here within the room, next to me and overhead. The odor of gunpowder became more acrid, more penetrating. Clearly, what we had always expected was now happening: we were under attack. Where were the police stationed outside the walls? Where the guards inside? Trussed up? Kidnapped? Killed? My wife had already jumped from her bed. The shooting continued incessantly. My wife later told me that she helped me to the floor, pushing me into the space between the bed and the wall. This was quite true. She had remained hovering over me, beside the wall, as if to shield me with her body. But by means of whispers and gestures I convinced her to lie flat on the floor. The shots came from all sides, it was difficult to tell just from where. At a certain time my wife, as she later told me, was able clearly to distinguish spurts of fire from a gun: consequently, the shooting was being done right here in the room although we could not see anybody. My impression is that altogether some two hundred shots were fired, of which about one hundred fell right here, near us. Splinters of glass from windowpanes and chips from walls flew in all directions. A little later I felt that my right leg, had been slightly wounded in two places.

To the uninitiated it may seem incomprehensible that Stalin's clique should have first exiled me and then should attempt to kill me abroad. Wouldn't it have been simpler to have shot me in Moscow as were so many others?

The explanation is this: In 1928 when I was expelled from the party and exiled to Central Asia it was still impossible even to talk not only about shooting but arrest. The generation together with whom I went through the October revolution and the Civil War was then still alive. The political Bureau felt itself besieged from all sides. From Central Asia I was able to maintain direct contact with the opposition. In these conditions Stalin, after vacillating for one year, decided to resort to exile abroad as the lesser evil. He reasoned that Trotsky, isolated from the USSR, deprived of an apparatus and of material resources, would be powerless to undertake anything. Moreover, Stalin calculated that after he had succeeded in completely blackening me in the eyes of the country, he could without difficulty obtain from the friendly Turkish government my return to Moscow for the final reckoning. Events have shown, however, that it is possible to participate in political life without possessing either an apparatus or material resources. With the aid of young friends I laid the foundations. of the Fourth International which is forging ahead slowly but stubbornly. The Moscow trials of 1936-1937 were staged in order to obtain my deportation from Norway, i.e., actually to hand me over into the hands of the GPU. But this did not succeed…I am informed that Stalin has several times admitted that my exile abroad was a 'major mistake.' No other way remained of rectifying the mistake except through a terrorist act."

Trotsky with supporters in 1940

Trotsky wouldn't be so lucky the second time around. On August 20, 1940, a Stalinist agent of Spanish origin named Ramón Mercader entered Trotsky's home and plunged an ice pick into his skull. Mercader later testified at his trial, "I laid my raincoat on the table in such a way as to be able to remove the ice axe which was in the pocket. I decided not to miss the wonderful opportunity that presented itself. The moment Trotsky began reading the article, he gave me my chance; I took out the ice axe from the raincoat, gripped it in my hand and, with my eyes closed, dealt him a terrible blow on the head."

Incredibly, the badly injured Trotsky was able to fight off his attacker with the help of his bodyguards, but he died the following day. His last words were allegedly, "I will not survive this attack. Stalin has finally accomplished the task he attempted unsuccessfully before."

The room where Trotsky was attacked

World War II

Although Stalin was worried about internal enemies throughout the 1930s, the rest of Europe was preoccupied with the Spanish Civil War and the rise to power of Adolf Hitler and the Nazis in Germany. Seeing this as both an opportunity and a threat, Stalin threw the support of Soviet Russia behind the Popular Front supporting the Spanish Republican government in the Civil War. Not only did he send tanks and aircraft to Spain, but he also sent about 850 personnel to man them and advise the rebels in their fight.

Stalin's main concern, like that of the rest of the world at that time, was Germany. Although the Treaty of Versailles that ended the First World War had placed limits on German rearmament, those provisions were routinely being ignored by the Germans, and European powers thus sensed their own rearmament was a priority. Concerned that Hitler would soon turn his sights on Russia, he began to put out feelers among other European countries about forming an alliance. Initially, his offer was met with skepticism. English Prime Minister Neville Chamberlain disliked Stalin and would have nothing to do his offers. On the other hand, Winston Churchill, who at the time was trying to rally his countrymen to the threat posed by Hitler, saw the practical benefits of the alliance Stalin was offering, saying in a speech May 4,

1938:

"There is no means of maintaining an eastern front against Nazi aggression without the active aid of Russia. Russian interests are deeply concerned in preventing Herr Hitler's designs on Eastern Europe. It should still be possible to range all the States and peoples from the Baltic to the Black Sea in one solid front against a new outrage of invasion. Such a front, if established in good heart, and with resolute and efficient military arrangements, combined with the strength of the Western Powers, may yet confront Hitler, Goering, Himmler, Ribbentrop, Goebbels and co. with forces the German people would be reluctant to challenge."

When Chamberlain visited Hitler in September of that year, Stalin became convinced that England was planning a secret pact with Germany against the Soviet Union. Thus, he decided to try to beat them to the punch. He contacted Hitler and proposed that they form an alliance, going as far as to fire his Commissar of Foreign Affairs, Maxim Litinov, a Jew who was an unacceptable ambassador to Hitler's government. Litinov's replacement met the following month with German foreign minister Joachim von Ribbentrop and on August 28, 1939 they signed the Nazi-Soviet Pact in which both sides promised to remain neutral in any future war.

On 30 September 30 1938, Prime Minister Neville Chamberlain returned to Britain and promised the British "peace for our time", waving a copy of the agreement he had signed with Adolf Hitler and Benito Mussolini in Munich the day before. Of course, Chamberlain and Munich have become synonymous with appeasement, a word that has since taken on very negative connotations, and war would explode across the continent exactly 11 months later.

Chamberlain holds up the Munich Agreement

From 1936-1939, Hitler took a series of steps in further violation of the Treaty of Versailles, but Europe still refused to confront him. The "appeasement" of Hitler by France and Great Britain before World War II is now roundly condemned, a fact Chamberlain himself came to understand in 1939, noting, "Everything that I have worked for, everything that I have believed in during my public life, has crashed into ruins." Before World War II, however, everyone still had to deal with the haunting specter of the First World War. Thus, most British people were jubilant when Chamberlain returned from Munich in September 1938. They wanted peace, and Churchill was seen as a dangerous warmonger and imperialist who was hopelessly out of touch and out of date.

Hitler

On September 1, 1939, the world was changed forever. Despite several attempts by the French and British to appease Hitler's Nazi regime to avoid war, most notably allowing Hitler to annex the Sudetenland, Germany invaded Poland on that day, officially starting the deadliest conflict in human history. For the French and British, the Nazi invasion of Poland promised war, and by September 3 both countries declared war on Germany. Meanwhile, the Soviet Union, fresh off a nonaggression pact with Hitler, invaded the Baltic. France and the United Kingdom, treating the Soviet attack on Finland as tantamount to entering the war on the side of the Germans, responded to the Soviet invasion by supporting the USSR's expulsion from the League of Nations.

Though Germany was technically Russia's ally, Stalin had no delusions that they were friends. Instead, he used this time to build up his forces for what he saw as an inevitable invasion. First, on the heels of the German invasion of Poland in September 1939, Stalin had his troops invade and reclaim the land Russia had lost in World War I. Next he turned his attention to Finland, which was only 100 miles from the newly named Leningrad. He initially tried to negotiate with the Finnish government for some sort of treaty of mutual support. When this failed he simply invaded. While the giant Russian army ultimately won, the fact that little Finland held them off for three months demonstrated how poorly organized the bigger force was.

Britain and France also began a naval blockade of Germany on September 3 which aimed to damage the country's economy and war effort, but the Nazis would blitzkrieg across the continent over the next year and eventually overwhelm France in mid-1940, leaving the British to fight alone. For the first two years of the war, it looked as though the Axis powers may very well win the war and usher in a new world order.

Initially, Stalin believed he had several years to build up his army before Germany would invade, figuring it would at least take the Germans that long to conquer France and Britain. However, when France fell quickly in 1940, it seemed he might have miscalculated, so he again sent Molotov to Berlin to stall for time. Meanwhile, Hitler trained his sights on Britain, turning his attention to destroying the Royal Air Force as a pre-requisite for the invasion of Britain. Given how quickly the Nazis had experienced success during the war thus far, perhaps the Luftwaffe's notorious leader, Hermann Goering, was not being entirely unrealistic in 1940 when he boasted, "My Luftwaffe is invincible...And so now we turn to England. How long will this one last - two, three weeks?"

Goering

Goering, of course, was proven wrong. During the desperate air battles that ensued, Britain's investment in radar and modern fighters, coupled with a German switch in tactics, won the day. The Battle of Britain was the only battle of the war fought entirely by air, as the Luftwaffe battled the British Royal Air Force for months during the second half of 1940. The Luftwaffe also bombed British infrastructure and indiscriminately bombed civilian targets, but Germany's attempt to overwhelm the British was repulsed by the Royal Air Force. British cities were targeted, and Churchill's very public tours of wreckage helped make him an icon symbolizing the determined, stubborn resistance of the nation. This was the first real check to Nazi expansionism. In reference to the efforts of the Royal Air Force during the Battle of Britain, Churchill famously commended them, stating, "Never…was so much owed by so many to so few.". And as only Churchill could put it, "Their generals told their Prime Minister and his divided Cabinet, 'In three weeks England will have her neck wrung like a chicken.' Some chicken! Some neck!"

Stalin knew that if he could delay an invasion through the summer of 1941, he would be safe for another year. Unfortunately for Stalin, Molotov's mission failed and Hitler began to plan to invade Russia on May 15, 1941. Since military secrets are typically the hardest to keep, Stalin soon began to hear rumors of the invasion. However, when Prime Minister of England Winston Churchill contacted him in April of 1941 warning him that German troops seemed to be massing on Russia's border, Stalin remained dubious.

Stalin felt even more secure in his position when the Germans failed to invade the following May. What he did not realize was that Hitler had simply over stretched himself in Yugoslavia and only planned to delay the invasion by a few weeks. Hitler aimed to destroy Stalin's Communist regime, but he also hoped to gain access to resources in Russia, particularly oil. Throughout the first half of 1941, Germany dug in to safeguard against an Allied invasion of Western Europe as it began to mobilize millions of troops to invade the Soviet Union. Stalin even refused to believe the report of a German defector who claimed that the troops were massing on the Soviet border at that very moment.

On June 22, 1941, Stalin had to admit he was wrong; 3,400 German tanks and three million soldiers rolled across the Russian border and headed toward Leningrad, commencing Operation Barbarossa. The Soviets were so caught by surprise that the Germans were able to push several hundred miles into Russia across a front that stretched dozens of miles long, reaching the major cities of Leningrad and Sevastopol in just three months.

The first major Russian city in their path was Minsk, which fell in only six days. In order to make clear his determination to win at all costs, Stalin had the three men in charge of the troops defending Minsk executed for their failure to hold their position. This move, along with unspeakable atrocities by the German soldiers against the people of Minsk, solidified the Soviet will. In the future, Russian soldiers would fight to the death rather than surrender, and in July, Stalin exhorted the nation, "It is time to finish retreating. Not one step back! Such should now be our main slogan. ... Henceforth the solid law of discipline for each commander, Red Army soldier, and commissar should be the requirement — not a single step back without order from higher command."

Certainly their resolve was tried during the first terrible months of fighting, as Germany surrounded Leningrad and then headed toward Moscow. The worst fighting, however, was in the Ukraine. Though badly outnumbered and destined for defeat, the Soviet soldiers held off the Germans around Kiev and thus spared Moscow while it was reinforced. They suffered the worst defeat in Red Army history, but were praised as heroes by their countrymen.

In September, as winter months approached, Germany continued to advance across the countryside. This led Stalin to implement his famous "scorched earth" policy, ordering the retreating soldiers to leave nothing behind that the advancing Germans might be able to use. He also approved the formation of small bands of guerilla fighters who would remain behind the retreating army and harass the advancing German forces. These two strategies, along with Germany's ever thinning supply line, created quite a handicap for Hitler's army.

To his credit, Stalin took a page out the Royal Family of England's book and remained in Moscow even when the city was evacuated and the Germans were only fifteen miles away. He lived and worked in a bomb shelter just under the Kremlin, acting as self-appointed Supreme Commander-in-Chief and overseeing every move made by the army. He bided his time and waited until November, when the German army was forced by bad weather to end their forward movements.

The Germans had reached the vital resource centers in Russia that they were aiming for, but the sheer size of Russia had enabled the Soviet Union to mobilize millions more to fight, requiring the Germans to dig in and prepare for long term sieges, even while the notoriously harsh Russian winter was setting in.

By the summer of 1941, U.S. entry into the war seemed just on the horizon. Germany violated the Nazi-Soviet Pact and invaded the Soviet Union, spreading war to virtually every piece of the European continent. President Roosevelt and Prime Minister Winston Churchill (another powerful distant relative) met secretly off the coast of Canada in August. The two issued the Atlantic Charter, a statement of Allied goals in the war. It largely reiterated Wilsonian rights, but also specified that a US/UK victory would not lead to territorial expansion or punitive punishment.

However, a substantial segment of the American public did not appreciate the more bellicose direction President Roosevelt seemed to be heading toward. Before the "Greatest Generation" saved Western Europe, many of them were part of the largest anti-war organization in the country's history. In 1940, the United States was still mired in the Great Depression, with nearly 8,000,000 Americans still unemployed, but World War II was the most controversial issue in politics. As the Nazis raced across Western Europe in the first year of the war, young students formed the "America First Committee" in Chicago, an isolationist group supported by future presidents Gerald Ford and John F. Kennedy. The isolationist group aimed to keep the country out of European wars and focus on building America's defenses.

The group expanded to include hundreds of thousands of members by 1941, staunchly opposing President Roosevelt's "Lend-Lease" act, which helped arm the Allies. The America First Committee remained popular and powerful until the morning of December 7, 1941.

Like with Germany, the Soviet Union had signed a non-aggression pact with the Japanese, but once the Germans invaded the Soviet Union, the Japanese no longer needed to worry about their border with Russia, allowing them to focus exclusively on expanding across the Far East and various islands in the Pacific. Though the Japanese steadily expanded across the Pacific theater during 1941, they were running low on vital resources, including metal and oil. In response to Japanese aggression in China and other places, the United States had imposed a crippling embargo on Japan, exacerbating their problem. Moreover, by winter of 1941, the most obvious target for Japanese expansion was the Philippines, held by American forces.

Ironically, because both sides anticipated the potential for war in 1941, they each made key decisions that brought about the attack on Pearl Harbor. Watching Japan's expansion, the United States moved to protect the Philippines, leading President Roosevelt to station a majority of the Pacific fleet at Pearl Harbor. Japan, assuming that aggression toward British targets and the Dutch East Indies would bring the United States into the war, decided they had to inflict a blow to the United States that would set back its war effort long enough to ensure Japanese access to resources.

Japan plotted and trained for an attack on Pearl Harbor for several months leading up to December 7. Believing that a successful attack on the Pacific fleet would buy Japan enough time to win the war, the Japanese decided to focus their attack exclusively on battleships, ignoring infrastructure on the Hawaiian islands. The Japanese also knew American aircraft carriers would not be at Pearl Harbor but decided to proceed anyway.

All Americans are now familiar with the "day that will live in infamy." On December 7, 1941, the Japanese conducted a surprise attack against the naval base at Pearl Harbor (called Hawaii Operation or Operation AI by the Japanese Imperial General Headquarters). The attack was intended to keep the U.S. Pacific Fleet from interfering with Japan's military actions in Southeast Asia.

The attacks took American forces completely by surprise, inflicting massive damage to the Pacific fleet and nearly 3,000 American casualties. Several battleships were sunk in the attack. Shortly after the attacks ended, the Japanese formally delivered a letter to the United States ending negotiations. Hours later, the Japanese invaded the Philippines, where American military leaders had anticipated a surprise attack before Pearl Harbor. Even still, the Japanese quickly overran the Philippines.

Roosevelt giving his famous speech on December 8, 1941

Roosevelt addressed Congress and the nation the following day, giving a stirring speech seeking a declaration of war against Japan. The beginning lines of the speech are instantly familiar, with Roosevelt forever marking Pearl Harbor in the national conscience as "a date which will live in infamy." Of course, the America First Committee instantly became a thing of the past, and the United States began fully mobilizing almost overnight, thanks to the peacetime draft Roosevelt had implemented. The bill helped the country's armed forces swell by two million within months of Pearl Harbor. In 1942 alone, six million men headed off to North Africa, Great Britain and the Pacific Ocean, carrying weapons in one hand and pictures of pin-up models like Betty Grable in the other. Japanese Admiral Hara Tadaichi would later comment, "We won a great tactical victory at Pearl Harbor and thereby lost the war."

The United States began 1942 determined to avenge Pearl Harbor, but the Allies, now including the Soviet Union by necessity, did not agree on the war strategy. In 1941, both the Germans and British moved armies into North Africa, where Italy had already tried and failed to reach the Suez Canal. The British sought American help in North Africa, where British General Montgomery was fighting the legendary "Desert Fox," General Erwin Rommel. At the same time, Stalin was desperate for Allied action on the European continent that could free up the pressure on the besieged Soviets. President Roosevelt had a consequential decision to make.

Roosevelt eventually decided to land American forces on North Africa to assist the British against Rommel, much to Stalin's chagrin. While the Americans and British could merely harass the Germans with air power and naval forces in the Atlantic, Stalin's Red Army had to take Hitler's best shots in Russia throughout 1942. But the Red Army's tenuous hold continued to cripple the Nazi war machine while buying the other Allies precious time.

In the dead of winter, Stalin ordered a general attack, ordering the Soviet army to throw everything it had against the Germans beginning on December 4th, 1941. The German army was caught off guard and soon driven back 200 miles. For the rest of the war, Stalin would be known for his orders to attack, attack and attack again. Because of this aggressive strategy, he was always in need of fresh troops, but it became easier to recruit willing soldiers as he demonstrated the German army was not the invincible monster everyone had feared. In fact, the Russian army's tenacity eventually became an inspiration for all the allied armies opposing Hitler.

Once the Russian winter ended, Germany once more made inroads toward Stalingrad, Stalin's own pet city. Not surprisingly, Stalin ordered that it be held no matter what. There was more than vanity at stake though. Stalingrad was all that stood between Hitler and Moscow. It also was the last major obstacle to the Russian oil fields in the Caucuses which Stalin needed and Hitler coveted. If the city fell, so would the rest of the country—and Hitler would have an invaluable resource to fuel his armies.

Stalin chose his best general, Marshal Georgy Zhukov, to lead the more than one million soldiers who would stand between Germany and the precious city. Stalin made sure that they were continually supplied with every sort of military paraphernalia available, from tanks and aircraft to guns and ammunition. He also took this opportunity to point out that his prophesy on the importance of industrialization to national security was finally proving true. Had there not been so many factories turning out weapons, the city would never have been held.

Zhukov

Zhukov, who had never been defeated, held the line until November 19, when Stalin ordered him to attack the now weary Germans. In a carefully planned pincer maneuver, the Soviet armies attacked from both the north and the south, carefully encircling the German troops until the German general, Friedrich Paulus, begged Hitler to allow him to withdraw. But by then the Fuhrer was obsessed with capturing the city that he refused his general's pleas, so the Germans attempted to hold on, losing thousands of additional men without taking the city. When Paulus surrendered on January 30, he had lost 1.5 million men and over 6,000 tanks and aircraft.

Entering 1943, the Allies looked to press their advantage in the Pacific and Western Europe. The United States was firmly pushing the Japanese back across the Pacific, while the Americans and British plotted a major invasion somewhere in Western Europe to relieve the pressure on the Soviets, who had just lifted the siege of Stalingrad. The Allies were now firmly winning the war. From January 14th to the 24th of 1943, Roosevelt, Churchill and other Allied leaders met in Casablanca, Morocco, but Stalin declined so that he could stay back and manage affairs in Stalingrad. The Casablanca Conference set out Allies demands for an unconditional surrender of Axis Powers. The leaders also agreed to the first major allied assault on Europe: an invasion from North Africa via Sicily into Germany. Roosevelt also agreed to increase submarine bombing in the Atlantic and to send more aid to the Soviet Union

Even before the British and Americans were able to make major strategic decisions in 1943, the massive German surrender at Stalingrad marked the beginning of the end for Hitler's armies in Russia. From that point forward, the Red Army started to steadily push the Nazis backward toward Germany. Yet it would still take the Red Army almost an entire two years to push the Germans all the way out of Russia. In July, just a few months after the surrender at Stalingrad, the Allies conducted what at the time was the largest amphibious invasion in history, coordinating the landing of two whole armies on Sicily, over a front more than 100 miles long. Within weeks of the beginning of the Allied campaign in Italy, Italy's government wasted no time negotiating peace with the Allies and quickly quit the war.

Though Italy was no longer fighting for the Axis, German forces continued to occupy and control Italy in 1943. The Germans attempted to resist the Allies' invasion on Sicily but were badly outmanned and outgunned, leading to a German evacuation of the island within a month. The Allies would land on the mainland of Italy in September and continue to campaign against the Germans there.

Stalingrad proved to be Germany's high water-mark against the Soviet Union. For the rest of the war, they were in a constant state of retreat. As the Red Army chased them out and retook more and more of the countryside, they were appalled by the treatment both soldiers and civilians had received at the German's hands. Over four million Soviet prisoners of war had died of starvation, sickness and other forms of mistreatment. In continuation of the "Final Solution," they had also killed all the Jews they captured, as well as civilians of any other ethnic group Hitler didn't care for. It seems that their thought process was that the more Soviet people they killed, the fewer they'd have to deal with later. It has been estimated that the invading Nazis completely razed over 10,000 Russian villages to the ground, slaughtering all the inhabitants they could get their hands on.

As word of German genocide spread throughout the Soviet Union it had a galvanizing rather than weakening effect. Instead of surrendering to the invading forces in hopes of receiving fair treatment, the Soviet peasants would hide in the woods when they heard of an approaching German army. From there, they would organize guerrilla groups that would strike at the Germans from all angles, picking off sentries, disrupting supply lines and spreading chaos.

Likewise, the Russian soldier knew that he had a better chance of survival in the field of battle than if they were taken prisoner, so they were more than willing to fight to the death.

Following the victory at Stalingrad, Stalin was gratified to be invited to join Churchill and Franklin Delano Roosevelt at a secret conference in Teheran in November 1943. Once ostracized by the now disgraced Chamberlain, Stalin must have felt vindicated as he sat down as a member of "The Big Three." However, his pleasure was short lived as Churchill and Roosevelt once more denied his request that the allies immediately open up a second front to drive the Germans out of Western Europe. Unfortunately Stalin's own success at Stalingrad had demonstrated that England and the United States were not as necessary to Soviet survival as Stalin had once claimed.

Of course, Stalin was no fool; he knew that these men trusted him no more than he trusted them. However, while his conclusion was correct (Britain and America disliked the Soviet system and would have loved to have seen it fall,) his concerns that they would someday sign a peace treaty with Hitler were completely unfounded.

In his defense, Stalin was at a disadvantage. He was something like the out of town stranger that someone had brought home for Thanksgiving Dinner. England and America were related both ethnically and politically. They also spoke the same language, ate the same sorts of foods and shared a mutual history going back nearly 1,000 years. Russia, on the other hand, was a mystery, a separate entity steeped in archaic tradition and mystery. Therefore, Stalin could not help but feel like an outsider.

Still, Stalin had no problem holding his own when it came time to talk of military strategy. Lord Alan Brooke, a British Field Marshall and Churchill's aid, kept a lengthy diary of the conference. This is how he described Stalin:

"During this meeting and all the subsequent ones which we had with Stalin, I rapidly grew to appreciate the fact that he had a military brain of the very highest calibre. Never once in any of his statements did he make any strategic error, nor did he ever fail to appreciate all the implications of a situation with a quick and unerring eye. In this respect he stood out compared with his two colleagues."

Ultimately, Stalin sided with Roosevelt and pressured the British into accepting a cross-channel invasion of France for the following year. Churchill was reluctantly forced to recognize that Britain had become the junior partner in the enterprise.

Churchill disagreed with the planning of Operation Overlord, but he lost his argument. Though the Allies used misinformation to try deceiving the Germans, all sides understood that the most sensible place for an invasion logistically was across the English Channel. The Germans had constructed the Atlantic Wall, a network of coastal fortifications throughout France, to defend against just this kind of invasion. Thus, the Allies devised an extremely complex amphibious attack that would be precipitated by naval and air bombardment, paratroopers, and even inflatable tanks that would be able to fire on fortifications from the coastline, all while landing nearly 150,000 men across nearly 70 miles of French beaches. The Allies would then use their beachhead to create an artificial dock, eventually planning to land nearly 1 million men in France.

During the first half of 1944, the Americans and British began a massive buildup of men and resources in the United Kingdom, while Eisenhower and the military leaders devised an enormous and complex amphibious invasion of Western Europe. Though the Allies theoretically had several different staging grounds for an attack on different sides of the continent, the most obvious place for an invasion was just across the English Channel from Britain into France. And though the Allies used misinformation to deceive the Germans, Hitler's men built an extensive network of coastal fortifications throughout France to protect against just such an invasion.

Largely under the supervision of Rommel, the Germans constructed the "Atlantic Wall", across which reinforced concrete pillboxes for German defenders were built close to the beaches for infantry to use machine guns and anti-tank artillery. Large obstacles were placed along the beaches to effectively block tanks on the ground, while mines and underwater obstacles were planted to stop landing craft from getting close enough.

Atlantic Wall 1942-1944

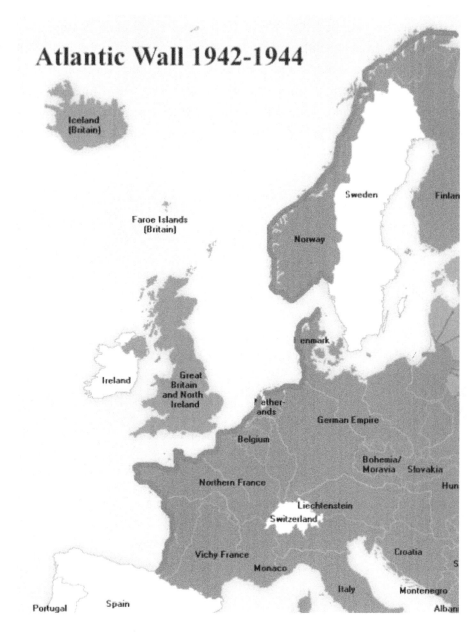

The Green Line marks the Atlantic Wall

Throughout the first half of 1944, France, once a lightly defended area used largely for the recuperation of German soldiers from the Eastern front, was now the focus of Allied and German attention, with feverish plans made for the region on both sides. Reinforcements flooded into Northern France while tacticians planned for the impending invasion and counter-attack. The speed with which Germany had reinforced and strengthened the region meant that the Allies were less than certain of the success of the invasion. Britain, weary of amphibious landings after the disastrous Expeditionary Force campaign of 1940 came perilously close complete obliteration, was more than anxious. Allied military fortunes had been, at best, mixed. Professor Newton points out Britain, together with its continental allies, had lost its foothold in Europe but had managed to bloody the nose of Germany in the Battle of Britain in the summer of 1940. The

Allies had lost Crete, yet stopped the Afrika Corps at El Alamein. With its American allies, Britain had successfully invaded Italy before becoming entangled in the costly German defense of the country. Britain, as a small island nation, lacked the manpower and supplies needed to singlehandedly defeat the German military. In comparison, the United States, an industrial colossus, had ample men and materials. Like Britain, American fortunes in the European theater were mixed, ranging from the successful landings in North Africa to the debacle of Kasserine Pass.

Storming Omaha Beach

Churchill was not overstating the achievements of *Operation Overlord* when he described the plan "the greatest thing we have ever attempted". On D-Day, the greatest armada the world had ever seen had landed 170,000 soldiers on the heavily defended beaches of Normandy in just 24 hours. More remarkable was the fact that the operation was a success on every major level. Deception, tactical surprise and overwhelming force had contributed to the establishment of an adequate beachhead. Confusion and dissent had stopped the Germans massing for any great counterattack. The Atlantic Wall which Hitler had placed so much faith in had been breached, and the race to Paris was on.

Operation Overlord aimed to have the Allies reach the Seine River within 3 months of D-Day, and it's a testament to the men who fought and served on D-Day that the goal was reached early. To do so, the Allies overcame firm resistance from the Germans, atrocious weather that limited resupply for the Allies, and the difficult terrain of Normandy, which included endless hedgerows providing hidden cover. And the Allies reached their objective ahead of time despite the fact the objectives of D-Day were not entirely met; the Allies had not captured Caen, St-lo or Bayeux on the first day.

Nevertheless, the landings were clearly a resounding success. Casualties were significantly smaller than those expected by commanders, and the significance of D-Day to the morale of the Western world, much of it under German domination, cannot be underestimated. For France, Poland, Czechoslovakia, Belgium, Holland and more, who had suffered over four years of occupation, the great democracies were finally coming to their rescue. American, British, Canadian, Polish, Commonwealth, Greek, Belgian, Dutch and Norwegian soldiers, sailors, and airmen all participated in the Battle for Normandy, which saw the Allies on the banks of the Seine River just 80 days after D-Day.

Sensing victory, the Allies began planning for a post-war world in the months after D-Day. In July 1944, diplomats from 44 nations come together in Bretton Woods, New Hampshire, where they established the International Monetary Fund (IMF). Otherwise known as the World Bank, the organization was aimed at providing funds for reconstructing countries devastated by war. The following month, the U.S., Great Britain, China and the USSR met at the Dumbarton Oaks Conference to begin planning the formation of a stronger League of Nations, this time to be called the United Nations.

After D-Day had all but sealed the Allied victory, Stalin's Red Army became more aggressive in retaking land formerly held by Germany. Concerned over the ever widening Soviet map, Churchill met with Stalin in October of 1944 (Roosevelt was by this time too frail to join them) and, while ceding Rumania and Bulgaria to the Soviets, insisted that Yugoslavia and Hungary be shared among the allies.

The sticking point, however, was Poland. Stalin demanded that the very anti-communist Polish government in exile be overturned in favor of a one more sympathetic to his regime. Churchill, on the other hand, felt a sense of obligation to the government as it stood, since they were hiding out in London. However, he wisely agreed to table the subject until the end of the war was clearly in sight.

In October 1944 Churchill met Stalin in a bilateral meeting in Moscow. He purported to divide the post war European states up proportionately, in terms of British and Soviet influence. Bulgaria would be 75% Soviet, for example. Stalin appeared to agree, but this was naive nonsense. Not only did it ignore Britain's diminishing role, but it was hard to envision how democratic Britain could share influence with an expansionist Soviet dictatorship within one given state. This scheme would ultimately be vetoed by the Americans, in an episode which further undermined Churchill's relationship with Roosevelt. Yet Stalin's apparent "acceptance" of Britain's suppression of the Greek communists in December 1944, seemed to accord with the deal and certainly led Churchill to trust him more than he should have done when they met with Roosevelt at Yalta.

The three leaders at Yalta

When The Big Three met once again, this time at Yalta, Stalin's home turf, the Allies were pressing down upon Germany from both the east and the west, and with the war in Europe in its final months and nearing an end, the meeting was intended mainly to discuss the re-establishment of the nations of war-torn Europe. Within a few years, with the Cold War dividing the continent, Yalta became a subject of intense controversy. To some extent, it has remained controversial. Among the agreements, the Conference called for Germany's unconditional surrender, the split of Berlin, German demilitarization and reparations, the status of Poland, and Russian involvement in the United Nations

By this time Stalin had thoroughly established Soviet authority in most of Eastern Europe and made it clear that he had no intention of giving up lands his soldiers had fought and died for. The best he would offer Churchill and Roosevelt was the promise that he would allow free elections to be held. He made it clear, though, that the only acceptable outcome to any Polish election would be one that supported communism. One Allied negotiator would later describe Stalin's very formidable negotiating skills. "Marshal Stalin as a negotiator was the toughest proposition of all. Indeed, after something like thirty years' experience of international conferences of one kind and another, if I had to pick a team for going into a conference room, Stalin would be my first choice. Of course the man was ruthless and of course he knew his purpose. He never wasted a word. He never stormed, he was seldom even irritated."

The final question lay in what to do with a conquered Germany. Both the Western Allies and Stalin wanted Berlin, and knew that whoever held the most of it when the truce was signed would end up controlling the city. Thus they spent the next several months pushing their generals further and further toward this goal, but the Russians got there first. Thus, when the victorious allies met in Potsdam in 1945, it remained Britain and America's task to convince Stalin to divide the country, and even the city, between them. They accomplished this, but at a terrible cost: Russia got liberated Austria.

At the same time, there was a sense of political change in the air. President Roosevelt had died and been replaced by the more down to earth and boisterous Harry Truman in April 1945. Also, while the conference was in session, the British elected the Labour Party into power, replacing Churchill with a new and untried Prime Minister, Clement Attlee. It is little wonder, then, that Stalin was able to gain such concessions, since he was the only one there who had been through the entire process.

Though the countries had often discussed Russia joining America and Britain's fight against the Japanese, it became clear at Potsdam that this was not going to happen. Instead, Stalin pleaded for help for his own country, which had been decimated by the fighting with Germany. Russia had lost more than 30,000 factories and so much farm land that the vast majority of the population was suffering from malnutrition. However, he failed to get much of a sympathetic hearing from Truman who, unlike his predecessor, was not particularly interested in the global picture.

Stalin was, however, and he was particularly concerned that the Allies might stage an invasion of Russia and overthrow his regime. While it may have seemed at the time that he was just being paranoid, we now know that George Patton was already pushing Truman and the other world leaders to go ahead and finish the weakened Soviets off. Thus, Stalin was actually wise to build up Communist governments in Czechoslovakia, East Germany, Bulgaria and elsewhere.

The British and Americans didn't see it that way, though. Instead, they assumed that Stalin was expanding the Soviet Union in preparation for invading Europe. The Europeans appealed to the Americans for help and with them created the North Atlantic Treaty Organization in 1949.

This mutual mistrust among all parties involved marked the beginning of the Cold War.

World War II was so horrific that in its aftermath, the victorious Allies sought to address every aspect of it to both punish war criminals and attempt to ensure that there was never a conflict like it again. World War II was unprecedented in terms of the global scale of the fighting, the number of both civilian and military casualties, the practice of total war, and war crimes. World War II also left two undisputed, ideologically opposed superpowers standing, shaping global politics over the last 65 years. As a result, World War II's legacies are still strongly felt today. In the wake of the war, the European continent was devastated, leaving the Soviet Union and the United States as uncontested superpowers. This ushered in over 45 years of the Cold War, and a political alignment of Western democracies against the Communist Soviet bloc that literally split Berlin in two.

Stalin's Death

At the end of World War II, Stalin hoped to continue to expand Soviet influence by blockading West Berlin, which was occupied by France, the United Kingdom and the United States. After the war, Germany had been split up into four parts, one part for each of the four major Allies, and though Berlin was in the Soviet Union's sector, it was also split four ways. The Western allies therefore had an enclave in West Berlin that was totally surrounded by communist territory, and Stalin then ordered a blockade of all supplies into West Berlin, hoping the other Allies would cede the city to the Soviet sector of Germany.

However, the United States and its allies were able to organize a massive airlift of supplies that kept the city of West Berlin supplied. Over the next 11 months, between June 1948 and May 1949 England, America and several other western European countries delivered thousands of tons of food and fuel to the city. The Soviet Union and its German allies eventually stopped the blockade when they realized the West could continue to supply Berlin by air indefinitely. As a result of their heroic efforts, West Berlin survived and Stalin was beaten.

Stalin's next great mistake involved Korea. Korea had been occupied by Japan and was ceded to the Allies after World War II. Without taking into consideration the fact that he had ordered his Soviet representative to the United Nations to withdraw, he persuaded North Korean dictator Kim il-Sung to invade South Korea. In 1950, communist Korean forces, with communist Chinese and Soviet support, invaded South Korea, which was supported by the West. The communist forces hoped to occupy all of Korea and make it a communist state

When the U.N. voted to send troops to oppose the spread of communism, there was not a Soviet representative present to exercise the country's veto power in the Security Council. The resulting war lasted over three years, and saw the United States military fighting communist forces in battle for the first time. The western forces almost captured the entire Korean peninsula until the communist Chinese entered the war. After much fighting, the two sides agreed on a cease-fire line at the original border at the 38th parallel. The cease-fire line created the border between western ally South Korea and communist North Korea.

Although the Russians were indirectly involved in the Korean War, the important result of the Korean War was that the Red Scare spread like wild fire through the United States, deteriorating U.S.-Soviet relations to an all-time low. In the decade that followed, it would become clear to the world that power was no longer divided among many little countries in the world but instead rested almost exclusively in the hands of the U.S. and the USSR. The Korean War was also the first example of America's containment strategy, which sought to protect non-communist nations from communist aggression to prevent the spread of communism to other countries. Containment would remain the primary American foreign policy strategy for decades.

When World War II was over, the United States and Soviet Union turned their attention from Nazi Germany to each other. Both sides began secretly working to recruit the Nazi scientists involved with designing the V-2 rockets and bring them to Russia and America, in effect giving them immunity from prosecution for war crimes. One of these Nazi scientists, Wernher von Braun, was instrumental in the development of V-2 rockets for the Nazis, and he was brought to America by the Truman Administration. Von Braun became more important than any American in the development of American rockets. In the 1950s he helped design the Jupiter class of rockets. When the United States fell behind the Soviets in the Space Race, they relied more heavily on von Braun's designs. When Apollo 11 lifted off into space, it was riding atop a Saturn V rocket designed by von Braun.

Von Braun

With the end of the war, American and Soviet scientists gained access to the plans and specifications of the German V-2 rocket. The two sides now had their hands on important, sensitive research, made all the more necessary due to the fact that their technology was well behind the Nazis' at the end of the war.

Even before the war, American scientists were experimenting with rocketry. Unlike the Germans, however, the Americans were unable to create a rocket that propelled into outer space. Regardless, the nation's scientists were actually the first to create a liquid-fueled rocket in Auburn, Massachusetts, in 1926. Four years later, the American Interplanetary Society was created in New York City, to promote the study of space travel.

Throughout the war, however, neither the Americans nor the Soviets were able to match the power of German ingenuity when it came to space exploration. With the war's end, the Americans and the Soviets seized the V-2 rocket components and specifications, sending them home to their respective laboratories for additional study. The United States harnessed the intellectual might of nearly 700 German scientists through Truman's top secret "Operation Paperclip", which stealthily relocated the scientists into America.

While the U.S. successfully brought in Nazi scientists, the proximity of Germany to Russia helped ensure it would be the Soviet Union that took much of the Nazi infrastructure left behind. Because the Soviets occupied East Germany, where much of the V-2 program was developed, it was able to capture and utilize the rocketry facilities. Quietly, the two nations began a race into space, using German advances as a springboard.

With these German resources in hand, both the Americans and the Soviets were able to project their own rockets into outer space within just a few years. Although Sputnik 1 will forever be celebrated as the first satellite to orbit Earth, America beat the Soviets in the race to project *something* into space. On March 22nd, 1946, the United States became the second nation in the world to propel an object into outer space when it successfully launched an exact replica of a German V-2 rocket outside of the earth's atmosphere. Later that year, the U.S. attached a motion picture camera to a V-2 and was able to take the first photographs and videos of the Earth from outer space. In 1947, the U.S. made great advances in using rocketry to transport living beings into space when in launched fruit flies into space aboard a V-2 rocket. Though they were just flies, this marked the first time a living organism travelled outside the earth's atmosphere.

Across the world, the Soviets were not so quick to enter space. The U.S. had the benefit not only of German scientists, but also of having German V-2 rockets on hand. It was thus much easier to copy the V-2 in America than in the Soviet Union, which only had specifications, blueprints and building materials. During the rest of the 1940s, the Soviets were playing catch-up on a variety of fronts, including the space and arms races. While the U.S. had detonated a nuclear bomb in 1945, the Soviets were not able to achieve that milestone until 1949, and while the U.S. now had a workable ballistic missile in the V-2, the Soviets would not have their own until the mid-1950s. Across the Soviet sphere, there was an intellectual disdain for space travel, which was considered impractical and irrelevant to the aims of the country, but space technology was vital for reaching military superiority or at least military equality with America.

When Stalin was first informed by the other Allied leaders about the existence of a new secret weapon, the atomic bomb, he had to feign surprise and ignorance about it. In fact, Stalin's regime had been working on a nuclear weapons program since 1942, relying greatly upon successful Soviet espionage to help lead the way. With intelligence sources connected to the Manhattan Project, Stalin was able to keep abreast of the Allies' progress toward creating an atomic bomb. By 1945, the Soviets already had a working blueprint of America's first atomic bombs.

On August 29, 1949, the Soviets successfully tested an atomic bomb, and with that, the Soviet Union became the second nation after the U.S. to develop and possess nuclear weapons.

The first Soviet test of an atomic weapon

In early 1951, the United States established "Project MX-1593", a top secret and heavily funded program that became part of the U.S. Air Force. The purpose of MX-1593 was to create an intercontinental ballistic missile capable of carrying a nuclear warhead. The aim was, obviously, to establish a system allowing the U.S. to target a Soviet site anywhere in the world remotely.

With Project MX-1593, America seemed to hold the advantage in creating an ICBM, and von Braun had been part of the Nazi team that envisioned rockets that could bomb the East Coast of the United States itself, which would have required an intercontinental ballistic missile (ICBM). However, the Germans were unable to achieve this goal. Since von Braun had already begun the research for an ICBM, the Americans seemed positioned to make enormous progress.

However, it was the Soviets who were first to create an ICBM. On August 21st, 1957, the Soviets launched the R-7 Semyorka, which was the world's first intercontinental ballistic missile. Work on the project began in 1953, while the American program had begun two years prior, but the Soviets were nonetheless able to complete the mission earlier. The first successful test launch in 1957 allowed the missile to travel nearly 4,000 miles.

Soviet eagerness to develop an ICBM was fueled in part by the superiority of the U.S. Air Force, which was larger and more advanced than the Soviet arsenal. Thus, the USSR felt it needed alternative ways to deliver nuclear warheads into American territory if its nuclear arsenal were to remain strategically relevant and military equity or superiority was to be achieved. The creation of the ICBM essentially negated the superiority of the U.S. Air Force, erasing all strategic edges the U.S. held over the USSR. At the same time, with this success, the Soviets opened nearly a decade of dominance of space exploration, which culminated in the launching of the world's first human being into outer space.

Among the major differences between the two superpowers was their leadership. While America gained a new and fresh president every 4-8 years, Russia had been under Stalin's control for over two decades. As his health began to fail, it became apparent that he had no intention of stepping down or even looking around for a worthy successor. In fact, those who were even whispered to be interested in his position often met with bad ends. Thus, when a rumor began to go around about a plot against his life, his closest associates panicked and began to make plans to leave the country.

Around the end of 1952 and the beginning of 1953, it seemed Stalin was on the verge of conducting another purge, starting by falsifying the "Doctors' Plot", which was to accuse Jewish doctors of plotting to assassinate top Communist leaders. In addition to being obviously anti-Semitic, it has long been assumed that Stalin was going to use it as a pretext to actually purge party leaders.

As it turned out, Stalin didn't have enough time to conduct the plan. He had suffered a major heart attack in 1945 and was suffering from various other maladies by the time he had reached his mid-70s. On March 1, 1945, Stalin did not come out of his bedroom, alarming authorities who finally entered his room that night to find him lying on the floor, seemingly having suffered a stroke. When he died the next morning, the official cause of death was listed as a cerebral hemorrhage.

Since Stalin's death in early March 1953, there have been a number of conspiracy theories suggesting that he was actually murdered. Ex-Communists and other political enemies have since claimed that Stalin was poisoned by Lavrentiy Beria, who allegedly boasted that he poisoned Stalin to prevent the coming purge. Nikita Khrushchev would later recall that Beria seemed ecstatic upon finding Stalin near death on the night of March 1, even while other party leaders were too fearful to take action based on the possibility Stalin would recover and take vengeance on them. Decades later, some historians continue to speculate that Stalin was poisoned by warfarin, a powerful rat poison that causes the kind of hemorrhagic stroke he suffered.

Khrushchev

The Politburo announced Stalin's death the next day, along with the new leadership. Malenkov was named the Chairman of the Council of Ministers; Beria, Kaganovich, Bulganin, and Molotov were named first vice chairmen. The new leaders moved against men Stalin had recently promoted to the Presidium of the Central Committee, and Khrushchev was one of the ones to suffer a demotion. He was removed as Party head of Moscow, and was considered the lowest ranking member of the Presidium. By September, however, Khrushchev has been elected by the Central Committee as First Secretary of the Party.

After 30 years under the absolute control of one fearsome figure, a power struggle was inevitable. The men who headed the Soviet Union were all intensely ambitious and, having survived Stalin, crafty, ruthless survivors. The Central Committee divided into factions, each looking at the other scheming to figure out a way to displace the other and avoid being removed from office.

Beria, Stalin's old head of security and the new leader of the country, was the first victim of the power struggle. For reasons that are still unclear, Beria instituted a series of radical (for the time) reforms, including amnesty for over a million prisoners. Khrushchev and Malenkov worked together to block many of Beria's proposals, and worked to pick up support from other Presidium members. These men were motivated by fear that Beria was plotting a military coup. Beria was arrested June 26, 1953, tried in secret, and executed in December; he was the last person executed as the loser in a Soviet power struggle, and in a symbolic way brought the final curtain down on the Stalin era.

Beria with Stalin's daughter. Stalin can be seen in the background.

With Beria out of the way, the question now became who was to take his place. Part of the problem lay in the structure of power in the Soviet Union. In effect, there were two governing structures. The government of the Soviet Union, headed by the Council of Ministers, was the official state structure; all members of the leadership were members of the Communist Party. On the other hand, the Communist Party of the Soviet Union, headed by the Presidium (Politburo) of the Central Committee, was in fact more powerful than the state organization. But in the power vacuum created by Stalin's death, each structure provided rival sources of power from which to consolidate control over the Soviet Union.

In this atmosphere, former allies Malenkov and Khrushchev became rivals for leadership. Malenkov used his position as Chairman of the Council of Ministers to try to give the government more power at the expense of the Party. Khrushchev, on the other hand, drew on his power base within the Party to try and strengthen the power of the Party and the Central Committee. He used his position to cultivate relationships with high Party officials and appoint his supporters as local Party bosses, who then became members of the Central Committee.

Malenkov

While both Malenkov and Khrushchev presented themselves as reformers, Khrushchev was the more charismatic of the two and also presented the biggest ideas, particularly in agriculture. Khrushchev's Virgin Lands Campaign to settle hundreds of thousands of young volunteers in Western Siberia to open up new areas to cultivation proved initially successful. Along with his reforms, Khrushchev had another weapon in his struggle against Malenkov—files from Beria that showed his rival's complicity in many atrocities from Stalin's later years. By February 1954 Khrushchev had replace Malenkov in the set of honor in Presidium meetings. Khrushchev's influence continued to grow as he won the allegiance of local party heads and saw his handpicked nominee appointed to head the KGB.

At a January 1955 Central Committee meeting, Malenkov was accused of involvement in atrocities, accused of involvement in the Leningrad case, and helping Beria attain power. In February, he was demoted in favor of Bulganin; Malenkov remained on the Presidium—as Minister of Electric Power, but from this point on, Nikita Khrushchev was the most powerful person in the Soviet Union. He would soon use this power to shake the very foundations of the country and the Party not just in the Soviet Union but around the world, by going after the figure most loved and feared by his fellow countrymen: Joseph Stalin.

Once he had solidified his power, Khrushchev next had to deal with the memory of his dead predecessor. Beria's amnesty program had resulted in thousands of political prisoners returning home with tales of the harsh, inhuman conditions in Stalin's Gulag. As rumors of Stalin's atrocities and abuses of power began to spread through the population, Khrushchev came to believe that the authority of the Party was threatened, since the true extent of Stalin's crimes was becoming known as more investigations uncovered more information. At the same time,

Khrushchev believed that repudiating Stalinism would boost the fortunes of the Party and inspire loyalty among the people.

Beginning in October 1955, Khrushchev began to fight to tell delegates to the upcoming 20th Party Congress about the abuses of the former ruler. He received opposition, particularly from Molotov and Malenkov, but Khrushchev persisted. The other leaders finally agreed, but got Khrushchev to agree to give his remarks to a closed session.

The 20th Party Congress opened on February 14, 1956. Khrushchev opened with remarks that contained veiled criticisms of Stalin. Nothing more was said concerning Stalin, however, until the end of the Congress. In the early morning of February 25, Soviet delegates were told to attend a special early morning closed session of the Congress; foreign reporters and observers from Communist Parties in other nations were excluded. What occurred over the next four hours was a speech by Khrushchev entitled On the Cult of Personality and Its Consequences. It became known to history as the "Secret Speech."

Before a shocked audience, Khrushchev systematically demolished Stalin's reputation. He began by stating unequivocally that there was no question about the late ruler's contributions in the Revolution, the Civil War, and in building up the economic system of the Soviet Union. But, he went on to say, a cult of personality had built up around Stalin, aided and abetted by Stalin himself; such a personality cult violated the very principles of Marxist-Leninism. From there, he moved to Lenin's own statements on Stalin: "[Lenin] detected in Stalin in time those negative characteristics which resulted later in grave consequences. Fearing the future fate of the party and of the Soviet nation, VI Lenin made a completely correct characterization of Stalin. He pointed out that it was necessary to consider transferring Stalin from the position of general secretary because Stalin was excessively rude, did not have a proper attitude toward his comrades, and was capricious and abused his power."

Khrushchev described the way in which Stalin proceeded to consolidate his power after Stalin's death: "Stalin acted not through persuasion, explanation and patient cooperation with people, but by imposing his concepts and demanding absolute submission to his opinion. Whoever opposed these concepts or tried to prove his [own] viewpoint and the correctness of his [own] position was doomed to removal from the leadership collective and to subsequent moral and physical annihilation. This was especially true during the period following the 17th party congress, when many prominent party leaders and rank-and-file party workers, honest and dedicated to the cause of communism, fell victim to Stalin's despotism."

While Khrushchev granted that Stalin did put down genuine threats to Marxism-Leninism in the Soviet Union (such as followers of Trotsky), he pointed out that once such threats had been dealt with, Stalin soon turned his sights "against many honest communists, against those party cadres who had borne the heavy load of the civil war and the first and most difficult years of industrialization and collectivization, who had fought actively against the Trotskyites and the rightists for the Leninist party line."

Stalin originated the concept "enemy of the people." This term automatically made it unnecessary that the ideological errors of a man or men engaged in a controversy be proven. It made possible the use of the cruelest repression, violating all norms of revolutionary legality, against anyone who in any way disagreed with Stalin, against those who were only suspected of hostile intent, against those who had bad reputations. The concept "enemy of the people" actually eliminated the possibility of any kind of ideological fight or the making of one's views known on this or that issue, even [issues] of a practical nature. On the whole, the only proof of guilt actually used, against all norms of current legal science, was the "confession" of the accused himself. As subsequent probing has proven, "confessions" were acquired through physical pressures against the accused. This led to glaring violations of revolutionary legality and to the fact that many entirely innocent individuals - [persons] who in the past had defended the party line - became victims.

Khrushchev then proceeded, over the next several hours, to systematically dismantle the Stalin myth. He detailed the repression of some notable Bolsheviks; questioned some of Stalin's decisions during the Second World War; and noted the many manifestations of the Stalin personality cult (place names, songs, etc.). He finished by stating, "Comrades! The 20th congress of the Communist party of the Soviet Union has manifested with a new strength the unshakable unity of our party, its cohesiveness around the central committee, its resolute will to accomplish the great task of building communism. And the fact that we present in all their ramifications the basic problems of overcoming the cult of the individual which is alien to Marxism-Leninism, as well as the problem of liquidating its burdensome consequences, is evidence of the great moral and political strength of our party. We are absolutely certain that our party, armed with the historical resolutions of the 20th Congress, will lead the Soviet people along the Leninist path to new successes, to new victories.Long live the victorious banner of our party - Leninism!"

At the end of the four hours long "Secret Speech," Khrushchev had succeeded in his aim—Stalin's reputation lay in tatters. Many delegates wept during the speech; some became physically ill; at least one person had a heart attack.   The shock felt by the attendees at the 20th Party Congress was soon felt across the Soviet Union and later the entire world. The speech was read the next night to delegates from Eastern Europe, who carried news of it home to their countries. Over the next weeks the speech was read to local party meetings across the Soviet Union.

In most places the speech was met by a mixture of confusion and relief; in Stalin's home republic of Georgia, however, the reaction was four days of rioting by Stalin defenders. The speech contributed to unrest in Poland and the Hungarian Revolution in 1956, both attempts to overthrow regimes instituted by the now hated Stalin.   The fact that all three reactions were violently put down quickly showed the world that, while Khrushchev was willing to destroy Stalin's reputation and reverse some of the more repressive aspects of Soviet Communism, he would not tolerate open attempts to overthrow communism where it then existed.

Even with the suppression of violent dissent, Khrushchev's speech did result in the first cracks in what, up to that time, seemed to be the monolithic Communist Bloc. Both Albania and the Chinese Communist regime saw Khrushchev's speech as a betrayal of real Marxism-Leninism as perfected by Stalin. Both countries broke with the Soviet Union and went on their own Communist paths, Albania to an intensely isolationist form of Stalinism, and China to a Marxist-Leninist-Stalinist ideology with the teachings of Mao mixed in.

While the short term effects of the speech were limited within the Soviet Union, the generation of the Secret Speech became the generation that, under Mikhael Gorbachev, would lead ultimately to the collapse of the Soviet Union and its allies in Eastern Europe. In the short term, however, Khrushchev moved to continue to consolidate his power within the Soviet Union. Unlike Stalin, Khrushchev also saw that it was important for the survival of Communism within one country for the Soviet Union to engage with the West—sometimes diplomatically, sometimes forcefully. For Khrushchev, that meant the United States.

For all of his prominence and power within the Soviet Union, Khrushchev was a virtual unknown in the outside world, and the West was less than impressed to say the least. Looking at the short, heavyset Russian who wore ill-fitting suits, Khrushchev was dismissed as a buffoon. British Foreign Secretary Harold Macmillan labeled him a "fat, vulgar man" and predicted he would not last long.

However, the "buffoon" soon showed the West he was not to be trifled with. At every turn, Khrushchev took the tactic of confrontation over conciliation. A believer in the ultimate superiority of the Soviet System, Khrushchev wanted to position the Soviet Union as a player on the world stage, an equal to the Western Allies—particularly the United States. His view was summarized in a statement made to Western diplomats at the Polish Embassy in Moscow: "We will bury you." Khrushchev didn't appear to be engaging in hyperbole either; the statement came as Soviet forces were crushing an uprising in Hungary that led to the deaths of nearly 4,000 Hungarians.

This confrontational persona was quite at odds with how Khrushchev would later be described by a biographer ("He could be charming or vulgar, ebullient or sullen, he was given to public displays of rage (often contrived) and to soaring hyperbole in his rhetoric. But whatever he was, however he came across, he was more human than his predecessor or even than most of his foreign counterparts, and for much of the world that was enough to make the USSR seem less mysterious or menacing.").

Khrushchev aimed to directly challenge the United States militarily, ardent in the belief that more nuclear missiles would help defend the Soviet Union. He turned away from conventional ground forces and a large ocean-going navy and increased production of missiles. Soviet eagerness to develop an ICBM was fueled in part by the superiority of the U.S. Air Force, which was larger and more advanced than the Soviet arsenal. Thus, the USSR felt it needed alternative ways to deliver nuclear warheads into American territory if its nuclear arsenal were to remain strategically relevant and military equity or superiority was to be achieved. The creation of the ICBM essentially negated the superiority of the U.S. Air Force, erasing all strategic edges the U.S. held over the USSR. At the same time, with this success, the Soviets opened nearly a decade of dominance of space exploration, which culminated in the launching of the world's first human being into outer space.

Khrushchev also spurred on the Soviet space program which, unknown to the rest of the world, was actually making great strides. The Soviets had few missiles in spite of Khrushchev's public boasting of a large and varied ballistic missile program. While the world was skeptical, one event changed that into real fear and concern: the launch of Sputnik.

By the late 1950s, what was previously a race to deliver nuclear arms using space became a race for admission into space alone. Although the 1940s and early 1950s were necessarily dominated by a quest to create rockets for military use, the latter half of the 1950s saw the science and technology fueling the Space Race being advanced as part of a competition for political prestige between the two ideological adversaries.

Dovetailing off their ICBM success, the Soviets were the first to make enormous advances in actual space exploration. On the night of October 4, 1957, the Soviets prepared to launch "Object D" atop one of its R-7 rockets. As the world's first ICBMs, R-7 rockets were built primarily to carry nuclear warheads, but "Object D" was a far different payload. "Object D" and the R-7 rocket launched from a hastily constructed launch pad, and within minutes it entered orbit. It took that object, now more famously known as Sputnik-1, about 90 minutes to complete its orbit around the Earth, speeding along at 18,000 miles per hour while transmitting a distinct beeping noise by radio.

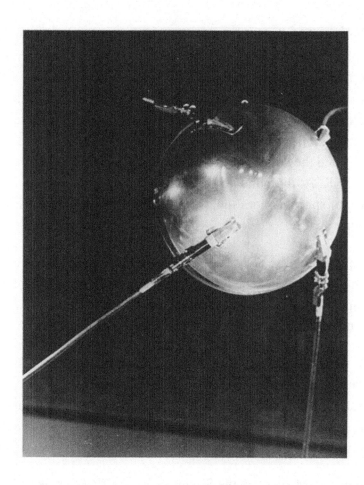

Sputnik-1, picture courtesy of NASA

Thanks to its transmission, and the bright mark it created in nighttime skies across the world, the world was already aware of the launch and orbit of Sputnik-1 before the Soviets formally announced the successful launch and orbit of their satellite. Naturally, the West wasn't thrilled to learn about the Soviets' launch of the first artificial object into Earth's orbit. Sputnik-1 could be measured in inches, but that large rocket it was attached to could wreak havoc if equipped with a nuclear warhead. Moreover, if Americans could see Sputnik-1, they were justifiably worried Sputnik-1 could see them.

The launch of Sputnik I is largely hailed as the opening moment of the true "Space Race", in part because of the fame and fear inspired by the launch, but also because its purpose was not entirely one of military value. While the Sputnik satellite indicated the Soviets had significant military advantages in potentially weaponizing space, Sputnik's value was not exclusively military. Internationally, the political reaction to the Sputnik launch was muted. President Eisenhower's White House was largely dismissive of the success, refusing to acknowledge its significance. Eisenhower played down the satellite, saying it was no surprise.

In truth, President Eisenhower immediately realized the implications posed by the Soviets' successful launch, and Sputnik-1 was a huge propaganda victory for the Soviets, who could boast not only of accomplishing the historic first but of getting ahead of the Americans in the Space Race. Had something like Sputnik-1 been America's goal in 1957, it very likely could have accomplished this important first. Von Braun had successfully designed the Jupiter-C rocket by 1956, which could have allowed the United States to launch a satellite like Sputnik-1 into space a year before the Soviets did. At the time, however, the technology was being designed for use as missiles. In response to Sputnik-1, Eisenhower quickly ordered an attempt to put a satellite in orbit.

From a political standpoint, the success of Sputnik helped convince the world that Khrushchev was willing to walk the walk, not just talk the talk. This led to political and policy ramifications in the United States; a major theme in the late 1950s, and particularly in the 1960 election, was the "missile gap", a gap which, when combined with the Space Race, provided politicians on both sides of the political spectrum in the United States with an argument to increase federal spending in research and development, science and technology education, and the creation of a space program. All this occurred as a public response to the new Soviet threat; privately, the United States knew, thanks to overflights of the U-2 spy planes, that the Soviet missile and space programs were less advanced than the bellicose Khrushchev indicated in speech after speech.

One of the things that occurred as a result of the Secret Speech was a greater openness to the West. For the first time, Khrushchev allowed American tourists to come into the country; likewise, he allowed limited numbers of Soviet citizens to travel in the West. He was particularly interested in trade and cultural ties; believing as he did in the inherent superiority of the Socialist system, he wanted the West to see Soviet achievements, and Soviets to see that their country was at least the equal to the West and would soon surpass it.

As a part of this opening to the West, Khrushchev was visited by then Vice President Richard M. Nixon in 1959. Nixon was the highest-ranking U.S. official to visit the world's first Communist superpower. In those years, Nixon (who as President would spearhead a series of policies known as Détente that would ease the rhetoric of the Cold War) was known as a leading anti-communist who successfully led the charge against Alger Hiss. This visit became famous for the "Kitchen Debate". In a model kitchen at the American National Exhibition in Moscow, Nixon and Khrushchev engaged in a spirited argument wherein each defended the other's economic system. Nixon's visit prompted an invitation to Khrushchev to visit the United States.

Khrushchev became the first Soviet leader to visit the leader of the Free World in September of 1959. For 13 days, he toured the country, fueling a media frenzy. Landing at Washington D.C. with his wife Nina Petrovna and his adult children, he proceeded to visit New York City, Los Angeles, San Francisco, Iowa, Pittsburgh, and Washington. Unfortunately for the premier, a visit to Disneyland had to be cancelled for security reasons. The trip ended with a meeting with President Eisenhower at Camp David, where the two leaders agreed to hold a four-power summit on Berlin to settle the issues on the city. Khrushchev left the U.S. considering his visit a success, believing he had developed a strong relationship with Eisenhower, who did not feel the same way. Regardless, the U.S. President was scheduled to visit Moscow in 1960.

It was a visit that was to not to take place. On May 1, 1960 Soviet surface-to-air missiles shot down a U-2 spy plane piloted by Francis Gary Powers. The flights, which had long angered the Soviets, had been resumed after a long halt. Khrushchev held off announcing the shoot down until May 5, worried that the incident would jeopardize the 4 power summit scheduled for May 15. When the announcement was made, Khrushchev tried to blame the overflights on rogue elements in the US military, trying to deflect possible blame from Eisenhower. The President, however, admitted that the flights had occurred and that he had ordered them. This put Khrushchev in a very difficult position with the summit approaching.

Gary Powers (right) in front of a U-2

The Paris Summit was disaster for Khrushchev. When he arrived, he demanded an apology from Eisenhower and a promise of no more U-2 over flights. He got no apology, but Eisenhower had already suspended the flights and offered his Open Skies proposal for mutual overflight rights. Khrushchev refused, and left the summit, and Eisenhower's visit to the Soviet Union was cancelled.

The collapse of the Paris Summit ended Khrushchev's "soft approach" to the West. In his September 1960 visit to the U.N. General Assembly, he showed his "hard approach". Rather than trying to charm the West, he began the Soviet Union's wooing of the new Third-World countries in an effort to bring them into the Soviet orbit. Of course, that effort was largely forgotten by Khrushchev's personal histrionics. During a speech by a Filipino delegate criticizing the Soviet Union for decrying colonialism while engaging in it, he took off his shoe and began banging it repeatedly on his table while calling the speaker a "jerk, stooge, and lackey", and "a toady of American imperialism". When the Romanian Foreign Vice-Minister began vocally attacking the Filipino delegate, his microphone was cut off, leading to jeers among Eastern bloc members. his microphone was eventually shut off, prompting a chorus of shouts and jeers from the Eastern Bloc delegations. The meeting was immediately adjourned, with Assembly President Frederick Boland slamming his gavel down so hard that the head broke off and went flying.

Khrushchev at the U.N. in September 1960

After the disaster of the Paris Summit and his performance at the U.N. General Assembly, Khrushchev hoped for a new beginning with the United States with the election of John F. Kennedy as the new U.S. President. Khrushchev saw Kennedy as a more likely partner in achieving an easing of tensions than the defeated Nixon; but once again, Khrushchev misjudged yet another American President. What Khrushchev did not know (or if he knew, ignored) was that the new President was himself an anti-communist who had little interest in "détente" with the Soviet Union. Kennedy's first few months in office were marked by tough talk.

Within just a month of becoming President, the issue of communist Cuba became central to the Kennedy Presidency. On February 3rd, 1961, President Kennedy called for a plan to support

Cuban refugees in the U.S. A month later, Kennedy created the Peace Corps, a program that trained young American volunteers to help with economic and community development in poor countries. Both programs were integral pieces of the Cold War: each was an attempt to align disadvantaged groups abroad with the United State and the West, against the Soviet Union and its Communist satellites.

Cuba and the Cold War boiled over in April, when the Kennedy Administration moved beyond soft measures to direct action. From April 17-20, 1,400 CIA-trained Cuban exiles landed on the beaches of Western Cuba in an attempt to overthrow Fidel Castro. This plan, which Kennedy called the "Bay of Pigs," had been originally drafted by the Eisenhower Administration. The exiles landed in Cuba and were expected to be greeted by anti-Castro forces within the country. After this, the US was to provide air reinforcement to the rebels, and the Castro regime would slowly be overthrown.

By April 19th, however, it became increasingly clear to Kennedy that the invasion would not work. The exiles were not, as expected, greeted by anti-Castro forces. Instead, the Cuban government captured or killed all of the invaders. No U.S. air reinforcement was ever provided, flummoxing both the exiles and American military commanders. The Bay of Pigs had been an unmitigated disaster.

On April 21st, in a White House press conference, President Kennedy accepted full responsibility for the failure, which had irreparably damaged Cuban-American relations. From then on, Fidel Castro remained wary of a U.S. invasion, which would have serious implications when the USSR began planning to move missiles into Cuba, precipitating another crisis a year and a half later. Between April and the following year, the U.S. and Cuba negotiated the release of the imprisoned exiles, who were finally released in December of 1962, in exchange for $55.5 million dollars worth of food and medicine.

Just months into his Presidency, Kennedy was severely embarrassed. Hailed as a foreign policy expert with heroic military experience during the campaign, Kennedy's ability to conduct American foreign policy was now firmly in question, and it would be eagerly put to the test by Khrushchev.

Unfortunately for the young president, April 1961 also witnessed the first manned space flight by Soviet cosmonaut Yuri Gagarin, handing the Soviets two propaganda victories. But the embarrassment of the failure in Cuba stiffened Kennedy's resolve not to make any concessions to the Soviets at the Vienna Summit on June 3, 1961. In their first and only face-to-face meeting (and the last meeting between a Soviet Leader and an American President until Nixon), neither man was in a mood to compromise. They were at loggerheads over a four-power treaty to settle the question of the two Germanys and Berlin, and over an atmospheric test-ban treaty. Both men left the Summit empty handed, and Kennedy later told his brother Bobby that it was "like dealing with Dad. All give and no take."

Khrushchev and Kennedy meeting at Vienna

Khrushchev came away from the meeting still thinking he could push the young president around, but the failure once again to settle the question of Berlin put Khrushchev in a difficult situation. East Germany was pushing for a solution to the problem of an enclave of freedom within its borders. West Berlin was a haven for highly-educated East Germans who wanted freedom and a better life in the West, and this "brain drain" was threatening the survival of the East German economy.

In order to stop this, access to the West through West Berlin had to be cut off, so in August 1961 Khrushchev authorized East German leader Walter Ulbricht to begin construction of what would become known as the Berlin Wall. The wall, begun on Sunday August 13, would eventually surround the city, in spite of global condemnation, and the Berlin Wall itself would become the symbol for Communist repression in the Eastern Bloc. It also ended Khrushchev's attempts to conclude a peace treaty among the Four Powers (the U.S.S.R., the U.S., the U.K., and France) and the two German states.

The wall would serve as a perfect photo-opportunity for two presidents (Kennedy and Reagan) to hammer the Soviet Communists and their repression, but the Berlin Wall would stand for nearly 30 years, isolating the East from the West. It is estimated about 100 people would die trying to cross the wall to defect to the West.

Khrushchev made one of the most serious mistakes of his career in 1962. Still questioning Kennedy's resolve, and attempting to placate the concerns of Fidel Castro following the Bay of

Pigs invasion, Khrushchev attempted to place medium range nuclear missiles in Cuba, just 90 miles off the coast of the United States. Though Cuban President Fidel Castro warned him that the act would seem by the Americans to be aggressive, Khrushchev insisted on moving the missiles in quietly, under the cover of darkness. They would serve not only as a deterrent against any invasion of Cuba but also as the ultimate first-strike capability in the event of a nuclear war.

In October 1962, with the help of spy planes, U.S. intelligence discovered the Soviets were building nuclear missile sites in Cuba. The president officially learned of this on October 16th. It went without saying that nuclear missile sites located just miles off the coast of the American mainland posed a grave threat to the country, especially because missiles launched from Cuba would reach their targets in mere minutes. That would throw off important military balances in nuclear arms and locations that had previously (and subsequently) ensured the Cold War stayed cold. Almost all senior American political figures agreed that the sites were offensive and needed to be removed, but how? Members of the U.S. Air Force wanted to take out the sites with bombing missions and launch a full-scale invasion of Cuba, but Kennedy, however, was afraid that such an action could ignite a full-scale escalation leading to nuclear war.

Kennedy's brother, Attorney General Bobby Kennedy, served as a critical advisor to the President and a counterweight to the aggressive posturing of military brass. Though he had previously taken aggressive stances in Cuba, Bobby was one of the voices who opposed outright war and helped craft the eventual plan: a blockade of Cuba. That was the decision President Kennedy ultimately reached as well, deciding on a naval blockade of all Soviet ships to be the better option.

On October 22, 1962, President Kennedy addressed the nation to inform them of the crisis. He told Americans that the "purpose of these bases can be none other than to provide a nuclear strike capability against the Western Hemisphere." Speaking of the threat to the nuclear weapon balance maintained in previous years, Kennedy stated, "For many years, both the Soviet Union and the United States, recognizing this fact, have deployed strategic nuclear weapons with great care, never upsetting the precarious status quo which insured that these weapons would not be used in the absence of some vital challenge." Thus, Kennedy announced a blockade, warning, "To halt this offensive buildup a strict quarantine on all offensive military equipment under shipment to Cuba is being initiated. All ships of any kind bound for Cuba from whatever nation or port will, if found to contain cargoes of offensive weapons, be turned back."

Kennedy speaking to the country about the Cuban Missile Crisis

Beginning on October 24th, the US began inspecting all Soviet ships traveling in the Caribbean. Any ships carrying missile parts would not be allowed to enter Cuba. Additionally, President Kennedy demanded that the Soviets remove all nuclear missile sites from Cuba. In response, Soviet premier Khruschev called the blockade "an act of aggression propelling humankind into the abyss of a world nuclear-missile war".

With the announcement of the embargo, and possibly fearing another American invasion of Cuba, Khrushchev ordered that his soldiers there could use any weapons at their disposal, as long they were not nuclear weapons. For the next four days, President Kennedy and Khrushchev were engaged in intense diplomacy that left both sides on the brink. Europeans and Americans braced for potential war, wondering whether any day might be their last. During that time, however, the Soviets used back-channel communications through Bobby Kennedy seeking a way for both sides to reach an agreement and save face. With his intimate knowledge of the situation, Bobby personally helped the President draft the plan for negotiations with the Soviets, which included removing American missiles from Turkey in exchange for the removal of Soviet missiles from Cuba. President Kennedy had created a committee, the Executive Committee (ExComm), and Attorney General Kennedy was placed on that Committee, giving Bobby enormous influence over the President's decision during the defining moment of his Presidency.

Though the Americans were unaware of it, Khrushchev had already decided to ultimately back down and remove the nuclear missiles by October 25. Finally, on October 28th, Khrushchev and President Kennedy agreed to the removal of the missiles, under U.N. supervision. In exchange, the U.S. vowed never to invade Cuba, while privately agreeing to remove intercontinental ballistic missiles (ICBMs) that had been stationed in Turkey, near the Soviet border, under the Eisenhower Administration. Realizing how close they had come to disaster, the Americans and Soviets agreed to establish a direct communication line, known as the "Hotline", between the two sides in an effort to avoid nuclear catastrophe resulting from miscommunication.

While the world and history have praised Khrushchev for backing down, the Cuban Missile Crisis would ultimately lead to his downfall in his own country. Since the removal of American missiles in Turkey was kept secret, most of the world and many in the Soviet Union viewed the deal as a full acquiescence by Khrushchev, dealing him a political black eye. Though he signed the first test ban treaty between the USSR, the United States and the United Kingdom in July of the following year, his political career was already over, even if Khrushchev himself wasn't yet aware of it.

Brezhnev in the 1960s

Leonid Brezhnev was born in the Ukraine in 1906 and had risen through the ranks to the position of major-general as a political officer. He owed his rise in particular to the patronage of Khrushchev, and in true Soviet style, it would be Brezhnev who would lead the campaign to oust his old mentor.[1]

Brezhnev ascended to the top of the Soviet leadership structure ultimately because colleagues were tired of Khrushchev. Soviet bureaucrats were fed up with Khrushchev's administrative reorganizations, his temperament, personal behavior, and even bullying.[2] Khrushchev also made a number of policy U-turns that infuriated his counterparts, and Soviet hardliners were angered by his apparent pursuit of some kind of arrangement with the West.[3] William J. Tompson has argued that ultimately it was Khrushchev's personal style, rather than policy or approach, that triggered the move against him.[4]

While Khrushchev was away from Moscow in the early months of 1964, conspirators began plotting to remove him from power. That March, Supreme Soviet head Leonid Brezhnev began planning for a removal of Khrushchev from power with a bunch of other party officials, with the plot ranging from an arrest to a simple ouster.

The conspirators, led by Brezhnev, Aleksandr Shelepin, and KGB Chairman Vladimir Semichastny, put their plan into action in October, while Khrushchev was on vacation. On October 12, Brezhnev called Khrushchev and let him know about a special Presidium meeting to discuss agriculture, though Khrushchev himself now began to understand what was up. When he

---

[1] William J. Tompson, *The Soviet Union under Brezhnev*, (Routledge, 2014), p. 5.
[2] William J. Tompson, *The Soviet Union under Brezhnev*, (Routledge, 2014), p. 4.
[3] William J. Tompson, *The Soviet Union under Brezhnev*, (Routledge, 2014), p. 4.
[4] William J. Tompson, *The Soviet Union under Brezhnev*, (Routledge, 2014), p. 4.

arrived in Moscow, Khrushchev faced condemnation from Brezhnev and others for his failures, to which he didn't fight. That night, he explained to his Presidium colleague Anastas Mikoyan, "I'm old and tired. Let them cope by themselves. I've done the main thing. Could anyone have dreamed of telling Stalin that he didn't suit us anymore and suggesting he retire? Not even a wet spot would have remained where we had been standing. Now everything is different. The fear is gone, and we can talk as equals. That's my contribution. I won't put up a fight."

Thus, Khrushchev faced no other choice but to retire as both First Secretary and Premier. Brezhnev immediately replaced him as First Secretary, and Alexei Kosygin became the new premier. It has been alleged that Khrushchev had already heard of his fate before the plenum but nevertheless was removed at the meeting. This would set a precedent, as something similar would be attempted against Mikhail Gorbachev in August 1991.

Kosygin

From the beginning, Brezhnev's regime attempted to pursue a different approach, claiming to have formed a "collective leadership" with Brezhnev as First Secretary, Kosygin as head of government, and Anastas Mikoyan as head of state. Just to make matters more confusing, Brezhnev was part of a ruling "Troika" in the early years, along with Kosygin and Nikolai Podgorny, as Chairman of the Presidium of the Supreme Soviet. It would not be until the early 1970s that Brezhnev tightened his personal grip on power.

The collective leadership and Troika principles are important in understanding the direction of policymaking in the Soviet Union.[5] After the highly personalized rule of Stalin and Khrushchev, the country became a more faceless entity after the 1964 coup as the people appeared to be stripped of any individualism. Under Brezhnev and his comrades, the Soviet Union took on a new type of authoritarianism, and while the USSR's citizens enjoyed a more stable existence, they would grow increasingly frustrated by a grim life unaccompanied by substantial improvements in living standards.

   While Brezhnev's regime may have been less draconian than Stalin's, it was still suffocating by liberal democratic standards, and Brezhnev took a particularly harsh approach to dissidents and intellectuals perceived to be at odds with the regime. Although the Gulag, the system of forced labour camps in use from the inception of the Soviet Union, had been all but abolished by the time Brezhnev came to power, it morphed into a system of mental health and psychiatric institutions. Dissenters were often interned in these institutions and labeled insane or incapacitated as a means of silencing them at a time when mental illness was still viewed with a stigma in many countries. Although this occurred under Brezhnev's watch, it was particularly promoted the head of the feared KGB, Yuri Andropov. This technique was accelerated by Andropov, who wanted to achieve "the destruction of dissent in all its forms."[6]

[5] Vladislav M. Zubok, *Failed Empire: The Soviet Union in the Cold War from Stalin to Gorbachev* (The University of North Carolina Press, 2007), p. 193.
[6] Christopher Andrew and Vasili Mitrokhin, *The Mitrokhin Archive: The KGB in Europe and the West*, (Gardners Books, 2000)

Andropov

Brezhnev's regime used a combination of sticks and carrots in the domestic sphere, mixing repression with a more moderated approach to Stalin, if not necessarily Khrushchev. Some historians believe that this combination actually preserved the life of the USSR.[7] Dissent was certainly repressed under Brezhnev, and the result was essentially a Soviet society that largely conformed with expected norms, but the regime also utilized more subtle incentives such as privileges, encouraging or disadvantaging certain behavior. In this way, the Brezhnev Era was deemed to be one of "soft repression."[8]

Brezhnev was very typical in his approach to economic, industrial, and agriculture policies. His regime ran a command economy in which all major decisions were made at the center, and like other conservative amdinistrations, Brezhnev and his fellow Soviet leaders were suspicious of economic reforms, particularly those that promoted any degree of liberalization in its satellite countries in Central and Eastern Europe. This was especially the case for Hungary and Czechoslovakia, as well as "non-aligned" states such as Yugoslavia, and some of these would be forced to change course by Moscow under Brezhnev.

In keeping with its Soviet predecessors, Brezhnev's administration implemented "Five Year Plans." The eighth of these plans was launched in 1966 and was a good measure of how the Soviet Union performed economically under Brezhnev. The state was then at its military zenith, having been engaged in a ruinously expensive arms race in the 1950s and early 1960s, including stockpiling hydrogen bombs. This was the era of long and intermediate missiles, multiple-entry systems, and competition with America, and the Soviet economy had to fund the colossal expenditures.[9] The Soviet economy did indeed expand during this time, but the rates of growth were much lower than what a developing country would desire. If anything, it seems somewhat incredible in hindsight that Western countries were worried the Soviet economic model might prove a worthy rival or superior to their own capitalist approach. As Western leaders remained concerned, Brezhnev's 1966 Five Year Plan had to subsequently reduce its targets downwards on multiple occasions, and the communist countries became notorious for falsifying their production targets.

The Soviet leadership would focus more on access to consumer goods in the 1960s and 1970s with limited success, but the approach under Brezhnev did have some merits. GDP growth in this period averaged between 4 and 5%, which likely helped the leadership also managed to somewhat pacify Soviet society, and as a result of the hermetic nature of the USSR, the country could present itself as a real embodiment of socialism. This was in stark contrast to the United States which by this point was mired in a disastrous war in Vietnam and was riven by strife at

---

[7] William J. Tompson, *The Soviet Union under Brezhnev*, (Routledge, 2014), p. 94.

[8] William J. Tompson, *The Soviet Union under Brezhnev*, (Routledge, 2014), pp. 103-104.

[9] Vladislav M. Zubok, *Failed Empire: The Soviet Union in the Cold War from Stalin to Gorbachev* (The University of North Carolina Press, 2007), p. 205.

home.

Brezhnev in East Berlin in 1967

The 1960s was a decade of decolonization and independence struggles for the West, and the Soviet Union was ideally placed to capitalize on these as the leader of the socialist world. Indeed, many independence movements had left-wing inclinations that were often blended with some degree of nationalism, making them targets for both the United States and the Soviet Union. Indeed, regional hotspots that popped up because of those kinds of conflicts became the main arenas in which the Cold War played out.

In this policy area, the Brezhnev regime behaved like the Khrushchev administration, but less bombastically. When Brezhnev came to power, he was faced with several opportunities to support left-wing groups in the developing world, prop up socialist governments, and generally oppose the influence of the United States and the West.

The Soviets had kept a relatively low profile in the aftermath of the Cuban Missile Crisis, but they continued to support left-wing governments in Africa and Latin America, as well as insurgencies in South East Asia, central Africa, and the burgeoning underground movements in Portuguese-controlled parts of Southern Africa.

The most significant war of independence during the era, however, was in Vietnam. After compelling the imperial power, France, to leave in 1954, Vietnam was divided into a communist North Vietnam and a nominally capitalist, Western-aligned South Vietnam. It wasn't long, though, before a communist insurgency gripped South Vietnam, leading America to stp in and buttress the South Vietnamese regime. Moscow had initially been wary of funding the communist insurgency, no doubt out of fears of direct conflict with the Americans shortly after the Cuban Missile Crisis.

However, the policy towards the Vietnam War changed under Brezhnev. Financial and military support resumed, and it proved crucial in maintaining the insurgency and drawing the Americans deeper and deeper into the conflict. Kosygin visited Hanoi in February 1965 in a show of solidarity with the Vietnamese communists, and as the war dragged on, the United States increasingly sought Moscow's help to bring the Vietnamese to the negotiating table. The perceived leverage Brezhnev and his Politburo had over the Vietnamese, which in reality was mostly elusive, would end up being crucial in bringing America into arms reduction negotiations.

A key component of superpower relations in the 1960s and 1970s was the split in the communist world between China and the Soviet Union, the so-called Sino-Soviet split.

Mao saw in Khrushchev's attack on the Stalinist "cult of personality" an indirect attack on his own central role in China, and neither Mao nor Khrushchev trusted each other. Thus, the 1960s saw a split in global communism between supporters of China and supporters of Russia, and the United States hoped to take advantage of this split at a time when it was fighting an interminable and ultimately losing war against Soviet-sponsored North Vietnam. China, meanwhile, distrusted the Soviet Union's intentions in Asia and stood to benefit from improved trade relations with the United States. In the view of Henry Kissinger, Nixon's Secretary of State, the ideological differences between the country mattered less than their common geopolitical goal of weakening the Soviet Union.

Mao and Nixon on February 29, 1972

The symbolically potent visits of both Nixon and his successor, Gerald Ford, presaged drastic changes that would soon bring China closer to the United States economically as well as diplomatically. In Mao's final years, the political fortunes of Deng Xiaoping, an old party member whose loyalty was attached during the Cultural Revolution, began to rise, and he would ultimately succeed Mao in the leadership of China. In 1978, Deng would implement major economic reforms aimed at turning China into a market economy, and the Chinese economy would become closely tied to that of the U.S., as both a major exporter of manufactured goods and the largest purchaser of dollar reserves.

As leader, Brezhnev became preoccupied with the perceived threat from Mao Zedong's China. While that may seem counterintuitive in the context of the Cold War, Moscow and its version of communism was the subject of much opprobrium in China, and the two nations shared a border about 2,700 miles long. Making things even more combustible, by the mid-1960s both sides were armed with nuclear weapons.

As the split between China and the USSR grew, delineations appeared. "Maoism" was considered a radical form of communism, primarily focused on agricultural and rural revolution, and it was the model followed by many underground movements such as the Khmer Rouge guerrillas in Cambodia in the 1970s. The Soviets under Brezhnev, however, were considered more conservative, or orthodox, in their approach. Thus, a budding revolutionary group's decision to look to Russia or China for ideological guidance was a politically charged one.

In addition to that, both sides had issues pertaining to nationalism. By the late 1960s ,the disorderly, radicalized Mao regime was disputing the Sino-Soviet border, claiming it was a historical injustice and producing other maps to stake a claim for territory that was now part of the USSR. In 1950, China had invaded Tibet and has claimed it as part of its territory, and Mao very nearly did the same with the island of Taiwan, where the defeated nationalists had taken refuge after the end of the Chinese Civil War. Only American deterrence stopped a military takeover there. Likewise, Chinese forces had invaded Indian territory in the Himalayas in October 1962.[10] The Soviets, therefore, had good reason to suspect that they could be the next target of Chinese adventurism.

In 1968, the Soviet military massed along the border with China, concerned that the Chinese People's Liberation Army would cross the frontier as it had in India. A number of low-level clashes occurred before things escalated in March 1969, and an undeclared border war continued for six months until the Chinese caved in and the Soviets actually claimed disputed territory. Hundreds of troops lost their lives in the clashes, and after the fighting ended, the Soviets remained highly suspicious of Chinese intentions.

Given these activities, it might even be fair to conclude that by the end of the 1960s, the Brezhnev regime was more fearful of communist China than it was of the West. The Sino-Soviet dispute would be the weakness that American diplomats could exploit in the 1970s, bringing both sides to the negotiating table.

Brezhnev had numerous other foreign policy concerns when he came to office. One of the biggest was the insurgency in the Congo, a Cold War theater in which several sides were actively backing their own proxies. As with so many other of the proxy wars fought during the Cold War, instability began as the imperial power started to withdraw. In the Congo's case, Belgium left the country suddenly in 1960, reluctantly handing over power to a Congolese administration that was wholly unprepared for independence. Nevertheless, a genuinely popular figure, Patrice Lumumba, took power, promising a number of reforms in the desperately poor country.

It wasn't long, however, before larger powers took an interest in events in the Congo. The country contained huge repositories of raw materials, access to which was clearly seen as vital. Lumumba was murdered in 1961 after a coup by the Western-backed Joseph-Désiré Mobutu, and a civil conflict started soon afterwards and lasted well into the decade. The Soviets backed

---

[10] Tom O'Connor, "China says it 'cannot stand' another conflict with India", *Newsweek*, 19 June 2018, https://www.newsweek.com/china-says-it-cannot-afford-another-conflict-india-985033, [accessed 15 May 2019]

various left-wing groups and had in fact answered Lumumba's call for assistance after Mobutu's initial coup.

It would be the start of a long presence in Africa for the Soviets. By the mid-1960s Mobutu was struggling to grip power, and the left-wing challenges were indicative of the state of the communist world. Perhaps surprisingly, the Cubans decided to involve themselves in the fighting, dispatching troops and advisors supervised by Che Guevara.

Ultimately, Mobutu took power in another coup in 1965 and managed to suppress opposition shortly afterwards. A long-running insurgency survived, however, led by Laurent-Désiré Kabila. Crucially for Brezhnev and the Soviet concerns about communist challengers to Moscow's hegemony, Kabila's group considered themselves Maoist.

The conflict in the Congo would be mimicked across the African continent during Brezhnev's time in office, and Brezhnev's regime would take a different approach to these kinds of conflicts, trying to ensure it was not outflanked as it had been by challengers in the Congo.

The Brezhnev Doctrine

Brezhnev was innately a cautious leader who sought to retain the status quo, and this would have profound ramifications across the Iron Curtain. T

With communism as the official ideology in Czechoslovakia, Czech and Slovak nationalism were severely repressed, though the two constituent parts were permitted separate communist parties. In fact, during the 1950s, the country grew impressively despite its conversion to the orthodox communism that prevailed in the region. Demonstrations broke out in Plzeň in 1953 as part of the protests across the communist world (ostensibly against agricultural reforms), but these were violently suppressed. Anti-government sentiment was subdued for a decade until a series of economic and political reforms in the 1960s which would inculcate the eventual forces that would force Czechoslovakia apart.

Antonín Josef Novotný replaced Gottwald in 1953 as General Secretary of Czechoslovakia's Communist Party, making him leader of the country. Following the pattern seen in many of the communist dictatorships in Central Europe and Eastern Europe, Czechoslovakia experienced periods of some economic growth then stagnation. The 1950s were relatively successful for the country, but this fell back in the 1960s. Soviet leader Nikita Khrushchev oversaw a thaw in the economic and political straightjacket imposed by most communist states from the mid-1950s, and although the USSR reverted to a more closed model after Khrushchev was pushed aside in 1964, other members of the communist bloc experimented with reforms during this period.

In Czechoslovakia, this took the form of the "New Economic Model" in 1965, which made some attempt at broad-based reform, as well as some economic liberalisation. What started as modest reforms—essentially an attempt to increase economic activity—opened a Pandora's Box of pent-up frustration. The results would have a long-lasting impact on the integrity of the Czechoslovak dual-national project.

In 1968 Novotný stood down and was replaced by the head of the Slovak Communist Party, Alexander Dubček. It was an appointment that was to have far-reaching effects for Czechoslovakia, the Cold War and even the stability of the communist bloc. Dubček quickly set about building upon the faint shards of light promised by the 1965 economic reforms. In what was called the "Prague Spring," Dubček famously said that he was overseeing "socialism with a human face."

Dubček and his allies were essentially trying to reform the communist system through increased democracy within a one-party state, reducing censorship in the press, radio, and television by encouraging dialogue. Cultural exploits such as music, art and poetry blossomed, and Czechs and Slovaks, previously buttoned-up, suddenly felt emboldened to air their grievances. Of course, the grievances were widespread, especially in 1968, a year of revolution across much of the world. Students organised across the country in a similar fashion as others across Europe, and this liberalization grievously worried the Soviet leadership and other communist dictatorships.[11]

In retrospect, it was only a matter of time before Moscow intervened. The USSR and the Warsaw Pact viewed the Prague Spring as an existential threat to its influence in the region, and in late August 1968, the Soviets sent troops into Czechoslovakia to reassert control over the country. The Warsaw Pact forces were met with bitterness by the Czechoslovaks, who resisted the invasion without resorting to violence. Dubček was summoned to Moscow, where he was forced to explain himself in a humiliating meeting. He was detained in Moscow before being sent back to his occupied country and stripped of his authority.

The harsh response to the Prague Spring was met with both support and criticism from other communist countries. Nicolae Ceauşescu, for instance, then a reformer in Romania but later a megalomaniac tyrant, made a speech in Bucharest's Palace Square denouncing the invasion as a "grave danger to peace in Europe, to the fate of socialism in the world."[12] Ceauşescu repeatedly expressed his support for the Czechoslovak communists that very nearly put him on his own collision course with Moscow. The Romanian leader was cunning enough to use the crisis to his advantage by rousing nationalist sentiment for an unwieldy outside power. This would be a core driving force in the eventual decline of communism, as reform often became intertwined with nationalism.

Yugoslavia's autocrat, Josif Broz Tito, would be another who tentatively came out in favor of

---

[11] Jussi M. Hanhimaki, *The Rise and Fall of Détente. American Foreign Policy and the Transformation of the Cold War* (Washington DC: Potomac Books)

[12] Misha Glenny, *The Balkans 1804-2012: Nationalism, War and the Great Powers* (London: Granta, 2012), p. 594.

Dubček, likely because he was under pressure from his own domestic protests. Yugoslavia was in some ways comparable with Czechoslovakia, as both were formed at the end of the First World War and represented multiethnic confederations. Both had been invaded by the Nazis during the 1930s and 1940s, both initially were sponsored by Britain and France, and both were abandoned in the face of fascism. The governments in Prague and Belgrade were therefore highly sensitive to questions about their own security, and although both states were now under the umbrella of Moscow and the communist bloc, the passions of their people were quickly aroused when it became obvious that their autonomy was only superficial. Ultimately, however, both Czechoslovakia (explicitly) and Yugoslavia (implicitly) were forced to kowtow to the Soviets in 1968 and in the aftermath. This was to cause deep resentment, particularly for the Czechoslovaks, and the anger would fester for another 20 years before the Soviet Union finally collapsed. For Czechoslovakia, the nationalism that was stirred by these events would lead to a peaceful separation in 1993, but for Yugoslavia, it would result in the bloodiest conflict in Europe since the Second World War.

Tito

1968 had another impact on Czechoslovakia, and that was the constant issue of its alliances, the matter that had so animated the state's founders. Reluctant participants in the Warsaw Pact that had now attacked them, the Czechoslovaks desperately called for assistance from other communist countries, and even to the West. The major democratic powers all considered coming to Prague's aid, but all had their own imbroglios. France was in the midst of its own insurrection, and the French elite were terrified they were about to see a revolution. Also riven by strife, the Johnson administration in the United States was mired in the Vietnam War and desperate to come to some kind of arrangement with the major communist powers to extricate itself from the war. The last thing it wanted was to be drawn into yet another communist dispute. Britain was more self-conscious of its failings a generation earlier, so it offered little other than voicing support.

During 1968, Czechoslovak communists had shown themselves to be open to political reform. Alexander Dubček's reforms led to an unprecedented degree of openness and dialogue, as well as greater political discourse and freedom of expression. His removal from office in April 1969 was a hammer blow to liberals across Central Europe and Eastern Europe, particularly as the occupation elicited no response from the West or NATO.

After the Prague Spring, attention turned to other parts of Eastern Europe, notably in Yugoslavia. The environment of protest hit Belgrade and then other Yugoslav cities, including the republic of Croatia. Encouraged by the reforms in Czechoslovakia, protestors in Yugoslavia started with intra-leftist disputes before moving on to more nationalist demands. These were particularly acute in Croatia, where a historical sense of separatism was reawakened in 1968.[13] Huge crowds gathered in Zagreb, and other movements across the country formed cultural groups that became known as the Croatian Spring.

The tension between Moscow and Romania and Yugoslavia continued into the 1970s, but the Soviets did not intervene to quell protests in the two countries. The main reason for this was that the Soviets thought Czechoslovakia was a more acute case, whereas sentiment in Romania was less explosive. Yugoslavia was a different example altogether because the country was not part of the Warsaw Pact and therefore had some level of autonomy from Moscow. In addition, Tito had made some overtures to NATO and the West, so a Soviet intervention might have drawn a more serious response from the West than Czechoslovakia had. In this way, Tito managed to maintain some independence from both Moscow and Washington.

Brezhnev himself, a conservative to the last, appeared content with keeping the status quo, but the Soviet intervention in Czechoslovakia set an example to other would-be rogue communist states that Moscow would not allow any breakout from its sphere of influence. This became known as the "Brezhnev Doctrine," and it would last until Gorbachev made his fateful speech to the United Nations General Assembly in December 1988.

---

[13] Carole Rogel, *The Breakup of Yugoslavia and its Aftermath* (London: Greenwood Press, 2004), pp. 141-142.

Brezhnev in 1968

Détente

The Brezhnev regime had experienced challenges since coming to power in 1964, and it eventually sought some kind of accommodation – détente - with the West, if only to provide some breathing space before the next phase of the Cold War. At the same time, officials in Washington were urgently concerned with extricating American forces from Vietnam, giving both sides incentives to meet at a negotiating table.

The Cold War could broadly be split into three hot phases and two phases of accommodation. The confrontational phases took place in the late 1940s/early 1950s, the early 1960s, and the early 1980s. Two phases of accommodation took place in the late 1960s/early 1970s and the late 1980s.

In some respects, Brezhnev was well-placed to reduce tensions with the United States. A jocular figure in person, Brezhnev was a compromise figure in the Soviet Politburo and therefore more secure of his position than someone like Khrushchev. His opposite number in 1968, however, was far less secure. President Lyndon B. Johnson had made a series of catastrophic escalations in the Vietnam War, leading to a huge death toll and catalyzing constant protests on American streets. Earlier that year, Johnson had announced that he would not campaign for reelection, but negotiations throughout 1968 prevented further progress for him when it came to ending the war.

Even as the Vietnam quagmire continued, Johnson managed to negotiate the Treaty on the Non-Proliferation of Nuclear Weapons (NPT) with the Soviets in July 1968. The NPT required signatories to renounce the use of nuclear weapons and only develop nuclear power for peaceful civilian purposes. The treaty allowed the two superpowers the opportunity to maintain the nuclear status quo. At the same time Moscow and Washington sought to curtail the incredibly expensive and dangerous arms race that had persisted in the 1950s and 1960s.

In some respects, the NPT has been the greatest achievement of the Brezhnev regime, as it continues to exist today. It has not always worked – some states have avoided ratifying the treaty and others have withdrawn - but even as the number of nuclear-armed states has increased since 1968, the NPT has more than likely impeded the potential development of a nuclear weapons free-for-all.

In 1968, Richard Nixon, a staunch anti-communist, was elected, but he would completely reshape American foreign policy by appointing strategic thinkers such as National Security Advisor Henry Kissinger. In fact, Nixon would signify a more wholehearted embrace of the concept of détente.

President Johnson had been desperate to withdraw troops from Vietnam, make some kind of accommodation with the communists, and even use the Soviets as an intermediary, but the Soviets were in no mood to make a deal with Johnson, particularly if they could contain the conflict to Southeast Asia. However, Nixon was much more of a challenge to Brezhnev – upon taking office, Nixon held himself out as an unpredictable leader who would potentially stop at nothing in securing American interests, even entertaining the use of nuclear weapons. As a hardliner, Nixon commanded respect in Moscow that Johnson did not enjoy.

As a means of bringing the Vietnamese communists (and by extension Brezhnev) to the negotiating table, Nixon actually escalated the conflict in Southeast Asia in 1969 and 1970. The American pesident increased the bombing of North Vietnam and then targeted the border areas utilized by communist guerrillas, most notoriously in Cambodia. With a sometimes bombastic inner circle of foreign policy hawks, the Nixon administration did indeed give the impression that they were willing to escalate the conflict and its growing brutality until it had achieved at least some of its objectives.

As an ally of Hanoi, this created further difficulties for the Soviets, who were also competing with the Chinese for ideological influence in North Vietnam. Both sides also had to deal with the emergence of the "Non-Aligned Movement" in the 1960s, a group of mainly recently independent countries that wanted to avoid alliances with the superpowers, or at least pursue a degree of autonomy within their foreign policy. As well as being suspicious of American and Chinese motives, Brezhnev also wanted to dampen the appeal of the Non-Aligned Movement, where the old Soviet nemesis Tito had become a leading light.

The Brezhnev regime was reactive in foreign policy terms during this era, unable to set the agenda on any major theme, and it would be the strategy of the Nixon administration that would alter Soviet policy in the 1970s, ushering in a period of significant détente. The Soviet leadership had the benefit of not needing to seek a democratic endorsement from their population, in sharp contrast with the United States.

With potentially decades in decision-making positions, it might have been expected that Moscow would be able to think strategically in the medium to long term, but the most influential strategic thinker of the period was Henry Kissinger. Born in Germany in the 1920s, Kissinger's family had fled the Nazis, emigrating to the United States in the 1930s. Kissinger was a student of realpolitik, very much in keeping with the German political tradition, and as an academic in the 1950s and 1960s, Kissinger had formed a complex, if at times somewhat sterile theory of the Cold War. U

pon coming into office, the Nixon administration was faced with the urgent challenge of ending the Vietnam War. Kissinger believed he could do this while simultaneously reducing the overall tension in the Cold War and locking in America's rivals into a more sustainable international order. For this he would exploit what he perceived as the weakness of the Brezhnev regime: China. By the end of his time in office, he would exploit, if unwittingly, another pressure point: human rights. At the same time, the approach of Kissinger and Nixon greatly attracted the Soviets because it seemed to indicate the Americans had accepted the USSR as an equal partner in geopolitics.

In his own telling, Kissinger wanted to end the rigidity, as he saw it, in international politics.[14] The key was to undermine the Soviet support for North Vietnam, allow America to withdraw from Southeast Asia, and reduce the arms race. As mentioned previously, many in the West had not realized the tensions between the USSR and China as a result of the Sino-Soviet split, and the Nixon administration now sought to use this Achilles heel to wring concessions from Brezhnev. Kissinger opened a "back channel" to China via Pakistan, offering the prospect of talks. At the same time, the American table tennis team was surprisingly given permission to visit China for exhibition games against a Chinese team, becoming known as "Ping Pong Diplomacy." The trip, in the summer of 1971, was deemed a great success and was used to pave the way for a political visit, which Kissinger described as "rapprochement."

Up until this point most Western countries, under the guidance of the United States, refused to recognize Chairman Mao's People's Republic of China and instead recognized Taiwan as the representative of the Chinese people. Taiwan occupied China's seat in the United Nations, and relations between China and the West had deteriorated further during the 1960s as the Cultural Revolution escalated. Any political overtures from Washington towards China, therefore, would be seen as a major policy U-turn, but this is in fact what happened. First, Henry Kissinger

---

[14] CNN, *Cold War* (TV Series, produced by Jeremy Isaacs and Pat Mitchell, 1998)

traveled to China to meet the Chinese Premier Zhou Enlai, and then Nixon met with Mao in 1972, shocking the world. Furthermore, the two leaders agreed to end the estrangement between the two countries, shaking the Brezhnev regime to the core.

Moscow now feared that it would be geopolitically boxed in from all sides by a hostile West and a rogue China from the East. The Brezhnev regime feared that an "anti-Soviet coalition" was being formed, although in hindsight the likelihood of anything like this occurring between China and America seemed remote.[15] Nevertheless, Kissinger and Nixon's so-called "triangulation" strategy worked according to plan, rapidly bringing the Soviets to the negotiation table as well and Vietnamese towards a settlement to end the war. The Americans suspected that if Moscow brought influence to bear over the North Vietnamese communists, they were more likely to make some actual concessions at the long-running Paris peace talks. Washington had been seeking a meeting with the Soviets for some time, and although Moscow agreed in principle, the Soviets had been consistently putting off the date of any summit, with the Americans seemingly stuck in a never-ending quagmire in Vietnam.

This all changed once Nixon and Kissinger played the so-called "China card."[16] Kissinger's direct line to the Kremlin went through Soviet ambassador to the United States in Washington, Anatoly Dobrynin who he met regularly. In this way the two superpowers could frame the negotiations that would take place at the summit which was quickly arranged after Nixon's visit to China.

President Nixon visited the Soviet Union on May 22, 1972, becoming the first American leader to visit the Kremlin. Moscow had a number of objectives regarding any agreement with the United States. The Soviets wanted a reduction in arms buildup, a restriction on nuclear weapons, and a tacit guarantee that the nuclear status quo would be maintained. The Soviets were concerned about defensive weapons such as anti-ballistic devices that could neutralize their arsenal. They also wanted the Americans to back them against China in their intra-communist disagreement. The U.S. never truly supported the Soviets over the Chinese, knowing that this lever could reap huge dividends, but the Americans did agree to arms limitation.

The Moscow summit was a success for both sides. Brezhnev and his allies took Nixon and Kissinger to his country *dacha* (home in the countryside) and, along with Kosygin and Podgorny, berated them for several hours over their actions in Southeast Asia before seamlessly moving to high-level diplomacy and agreeing to a number of the key principles of détente. Clearly, the Soviets were enthusiastic to limit offensive and defensive nuclear weapons.

The positive outcome of the Moscow talks played very well back on all sides. Nixon was received as a leader who had reduced the dangerous levels of tension in the Cold War, and for

---

[15] CNN, *Cold War* (TV Series, produced by Jeremy Isaacs and Pat Mitchell, 1998)
[16] Godfrey Hodgson, *People's Century: From the dawn of the century to the eve of the millennium* (Godalming: BBC Books, 1998)

Brezhnev, détente created breathing space and some degree of stability in the Soviet Union and the wider communist world. China slowly drifted away from its revolutionary behavior, and relations between China and Russia gradually improved.

The most immediate impact of détente was on Southeast Asia. The Americans achieved their short-term goal by meeting the North Vietnamese more seriously at the negotiating table in Paris. The broad principles of a peace agreement were fleshed out during the rest of 1972. Hanoi, however, was reluctant to finalize the accords, which led to a wave of brutal bombings at the turn of the year by the Americans, the so-called "Christmas Bombings."[17] The callous, blunt instrument of aerial bombing served its purpose in American eyes. In January 1973, an agreement was reached between North Vietnam and South Vietnam, allowing the Americans to withdraw and satisfy public opinion at home. Tens of thousands of American troops and millions of Vietnamese had died in the conflict, and the agreement lasted just over two years until April 1975, when the communists overran the South Vietnamese army and forcibly unified the country. By this time, Nixon had been forced from office thanks to Watergate.

The most lasting impact of détente was nuclear arms limitation. Alongside the NPT, there would be two other major agreements signed between the superpowers. The Anti-Ballistic Missile Treaty (ABM Treaty) was signed by Nixon and Brezhnev at the Moscow summit, designed to limit defensive weapons that could neutralize either side's offensive missiles. Although counterintuitive in principle, the ABM Treaty was supposed to create a level playing field and ultimately deter either side from using nuclear weapons of any kind.

The Strategic Arms Limitation Talks (SALT) were a long-running series of negotiations that had begun during Nixon's first year in office in 1969 and based in the Finnish capital Helsinki. It culminated in the first SALT treaty, also signed in Moscow during Nixon's visit in May 1972. SALT sought to limit offensive nuclear weapons, intercontinental ballistic missiles (ICBMs), and other varieties of weapons launched from sea and land. It was a major step forward after two decades of nuclear weapons stockpiling.

The environment of détente also led to some degree of reconciliation between East and West Germany. Previously seen as one of the areas most likely to lead to a conflagration, West German Chancellor Willy Brandt, in power from 1969-1974, reversed the policy of his predecessors, which had been to ignore the East German state and refuse to deal with countries that recognized it. Brandt visited Poland and the Soviet Union, showing a remarkable level of contrition for the crimes of the Nazis and reaching agreements with the communist bloc. Most notably, Brandt met with East German leaders, and the two states agreed to reduce tension and improve relations, including family visits across the Berlin Wall.[18]

---

[17] Rebecca Kesby, 'North Vietnam, 1972: The Christmas bombing of Hanoi', *BBC News*, 24 December 2012, https://www.bbc.com/news/magazine-20719382, [accessed 14 May 2019]
[18] Mary Fulbrook, *History of Germany, 1918-2000: the divided nation* (Oxford: Blackwell, 2002)

Known as *Ostpolitik* in German, this local détente both satisfied and worried Brezhnev's government. The policy appeared to recognize the post-war status quo, including the acceptance of a Soviet-led sphere of influence in Central and Eastern Europe. Conversely, *Ostpolitik* worried the superpowers because it suggested an independent foreign policy in Bonn and Berlin, as well as the possibility of a reunified Germany and revival of German nationalism. This would indeed come to pass, but not until the next phase of détente in the late 1980s, and when it did occur, both superpowers embraced German reunification.

Brezhnev visited the American president in June 1973 and expressed utter bemusement at Nixon's domestic troubles around the Watergate saga.[19] In the authoritarian Soviet Union, scandals never entered the minds of the country's leaders. Although without the kind of treaty signing that had occurred the previous year in Moscow, Brezhnev and Nixon vowed to work together to further peace between the two superpowers. A little over a year later, Nixon was forced to resign, but the détente process continued for several more years.

Brezhnev and Nixon meeting in 1973

The culmination of the détente process was the 1975 Helsinki Final Act, signed by every European state and both superpowers.[20] It had been set in motion by the developments of the

[19] Robert Coalson, 'A Surprisingly Candid Chat Between Nixon and Brezhnev', *The Atlantic*, 26 August 2013, https://www.theatlantic.com/international/archive/2013/08/a-surprisingly-candid-chat-between-nixon-and-brezhnev/278981/, [accessed 14 May 2019]

previous years, the SALT discussions, and the high-level summits American and Soviet officials. Brezhnev himself addressed the 1975 Helsinki conference, highlighting the need for world peace through a new accommodation between East and West. Brezhnev, although by now ailing somewhat, wanted to present himself as a statesman and peacemaker. Indeed, since he came to power in 1964, his regime had overseen a better standard of living for the Soviet people and managed to avoid, by and large, the conflicts of his Western counterparts.

Ironically, with the benefit of hindsight, many historians have subsequently cited Brezhnev's signing of the Helsinki accords as the communist bloc's death sentence, lighting the fuse of a time bomb under his own country's existence. How did Brezhnev turn this apparent victory into a road to defeat for the Soviet Union and its system of alliances?

The Soviets were eager to conclude the Helsinki talks, which had actually started earlier in the 1970s, because they would effectively recognize the post-1945 borders in Europe. This held particular attraction for the Soviet Politburo because it appeared to accept the separation of Europe into American and Soviet spheres of influence. What is worth keeping in mind here is that for much of the period after the start of the Cold War, Moscow believed that the West was working to undermine its influence in Central and Eastern Europe, encouraging the revolts of 1953, 1956 and 1968, all while recognizing the communist regime in East Germany.[21] Helsinki would solve all these difficulties in one overarching agreement. Yet, the devil was in the detail. While the first two articles, or baskets, of the accords concentrated on hard power issues, the Third Basket focused on humanitarian themes, including the recognition of liberal values such as human rights. Pursued by the West Germans, the Third Basket was initially vehemently opposed by Moscow and also resisted by Secretary of State Henry Kissinger for the same reason: both Kissinger and his Soviet counterparts believed that the human rights provisions would introduce a degree of instability into the situation in Europe. That belief proved prescient.

Despite their respective doubts, the Soviets, Americans, and every communist regime signed the Helsinki Final Act on August 1, 1975.[22] Included within this third article was provision for a new organization, the Commission on Security and Cooperation in Europe (the CSCE), which would monitor both security and the values set out in the accord. By all accounts, it was long-term Politburo member and veteran communist Andrei Gromyko who convinced his colleagues to approve the agreement by outlining the importance of the border issues and recognition of the status quo. Gromyko believed that Moscow could override any concerns about human rights with the simple invocation of sovereignty.[23] The West had shown it was not prepared to intervene in internal communist disputes in Europe, such as in Czechoslovakia in 1968, so any commitment to values like human rights would be hollow.

---

[20] Gerald Knaus, "Europe and Azerbaijan: The End of Shame", *Journal of Democracy,* (2015, pp. 5-18)

[21] Mary Fulbrook, *History of Germany, 1918-2000: the divided nation* (Oxford: Blackwell, 2002)

[22] OSCE, Helsinki Final Act, 1 August 1975, https://www.osce.org/helsinki-final-act, [accessed 14 May 2019]

[23] CNN, *Cold War* (TV Series, produced by Jeremy Isaacs and Pat Mitchell, 1998)

This turned out to be a fatal misreading of the situation. The communists did not allow for the possibility that the populations in the communist world might take these provisions seriously, but shortly after the signing of the Helsinki Final Act, dissident groups cited them in their underground activities in Czechoslovakia.[24] Within the space of a few years, the language of human rights would be used from within to undermine authoritarian regimes across the communist world.

The Brezhnev regime was increasingly dogged by criticism surrounding human rights as the 1970s progressed. The criticism came initially from Democrat politicians and liberal public opinion in North America and Western Europe. These critics adopted several *cause celebres* within the Soviet Union, such as Aleksandr Solzhenitsyn and Andrei Sakharov, as well as Jews trying to leave the USSR, known as *Refuseniks*.

Author Aleksandr Solzhenitsyn had quite a history of dissident activity within the Soviet Union. He had served in the Red Army during the Second World War and had subsequently been a prisoner in the Gulag system, using these experiences as the basis for his writing.[25] He published his first book, *One Day in the Life of Ivan Denisovich*, in installments in 1962, surprisingly receiving the approval of the nominally reformist Khrushchev. His major work was published as *The Gulag Archipelago: 1918-1956* in 1973, but this time it was met with severe condemnation by the Brezhnev regime. What made things worse for the Soviet Politburo was that Solzhenitsyn had been awarded the Nobel Prize for Literature in 1970.

His name was increasingly invoked in the West to demonstrate the moral bankruptcy of the Soviet system, and it served accusations that the Nixon and Ford administrations were amoral in their pursuit of détente with such authoritarianism. The Brezhnev regime denounced Solzhenitsyn in January 1974, claiming he was a fascist and expelling him from the Soviet Union the following month. Solzhenitsyn traveled to the United States via West Germany and became a vehement critic of the USSR. The whole episode proved to be a propaganda disaster for Brezhnev.

Like Solzhenitsyn, Soviet nuclear scientist Andrei Sakharov gained international recognition in the 1970s. Sakharov criticised the Brezhnev regime on human rights grounds from the 1960s and was granted the Nobel Peace Prize in 1975. Again, this drew a hostile response from the Soviet authorities. After he demonstrated against the invasion of Afghanistan some years later, he was sent to a detention facility. His case became another well-known example of the repression used within the Soviet Union. Sakharov would not be released until the Gorbachev era.

---

[24] Emily Tamkin, "In Charter 77, Czech Dissidents Charted New Territory", *Foreign Policy*, 3 February 2017, https://foreignpolicy.com/2017/02/03/in-charter-77-czech-dissidents-charted-new-territory/, [accessed 10 April 2019]
[25] Aleksandr I. Solzhenitsyn, *The Gulag Archipelago 1918-1956: An Experiment in Literary Investigation,* (London: Harper & Row, 1973, translated by Thomas P. Whitney)

Adding to Brezhnev's list of headaches on human rights were the so-called *Refuseniks*. The State of Israel had promised citizenship to any Jewish person from across the world, whatever their existing nationality. Many Soviet Jews wanted to take up this offer in the late 1960s but were prevented from leaving by the Brezhnev regime. Their refusal stimulated the unofficial moniker *Refusenik*. The reason the authorities gave for this was usually based around a spurious notion of national security. As news of the refusals filtered into the outside world, the *Refuseniks* gained international sympathy, and it became another propaganda blow for Moscow.[26]

What made the situation worse for Soviet Jews was that they had been routinely persecuted by the authorities under communist rule, particularly under Stalin, so preventing Soviet Jews from even leaving the country added insult to injury. The Helsinki Final Act acted as a catalyst for human rights activists and something similar occurred with the *Refuseniks*. Led by Natan Sharansky, the *Refuseniks* protested in Moscow in 1976, citing the Helsinki provisions. The Soviet response to the protestors and figures such as Sharansky was familiar: a trumped-up judicial process and jail. Nevertheless, the *Refusenik* issue would not go away. President Jimmy Carter put the issue of human rights front and center and expressed support for the *Refuseniks*, infuriating the Kremlin.

The issue of Jewish emigration from the Soviet Union, as well as other human rights violations, led Congress to pass the 1974 "Jackson-Vanik Amendment." Authored by Congressman Charles A. Vanik and Henry "Scoop" Jackson, the law reduced the trading status of any country that prevented emigration or trampled on human rights. It was squarely targeted at the Soviet Union and marked the beginning of the end of détente. A process that had started with geopolitics and winding down the Vietnam War met a backlash had morphed into concerns over human rights, an issue where the Soviets were uniquely vulnerable.

The End of the Brezhnev Era

The Brezhnev regime may have come under pressure in the international sphere over human rights, but it had managed to quell domestic dissent by the 1970s. Many Soviet citizens were content with the status quo following years of turmoil and with memories still alive of the hardships and violence of the Second World War. But whereas Brezhnev could perhaps feel as if his regime had achieved tangible results by the 1970s, it was his slow response to change that really damaged his reputation subsequently.

Without question, economic and social life ossified during the 1970s. It was later suggested that corruption became widespread under Brezhnev during this time, but corruption is always a feature of one-party states.[27] Crucially, Brezhnev's USSR was inefficient - in keeping with other Soviet leaders, economic decisions were made by the central authorities through the Politburo.

---

[26] *The New York Times*, 'Remember the Refuseniks?', 14 December 1990, https://www.nytimes.com/1990/12/14/opinion/remember-the-refuseniks.html, [accessed 15 May 2019]
[27] Stephen White, *Communism and its Collapse* (Routledge, 2002), p. 67.

Moscow decided where to pool resources, how many goods and services were needed, and what levels of production were targeted. It was a classic version of a command economy that led seamlessly to stagnation because the Soviet economy lacked dynamism.[28] Without rewards or even private property, the Soviet people were disincentivized against increasing productivity. According to outside estimates the Soviet economy slowed drastically in the second half of the 1970s, essentially unable to recover for the rest of the USSR's existence.[29]

Similarly, the political system was so hermetically sealed that many citizens resigned themselves to the fact that they could not change the system or freely speak their minds. Yuri Andropov had indeed achieved his aim to crush dissent.

Nevertheless, a compact of sorts developed under Brezhnev.[30] The Soviet people would not air any grievances in public or criticise the authorities or their political masters. Behind closed doors, however, they would freely lambast the failings of the communist regime.

As for alcohol consumption, it was indeed very high during the Brezhnev Era and this has been linked with wider dissatisfaction regarding the Soviet system.[31] Historians have suggested that leaders such as Brezhnev did not want to crackdown on alcohol use because it acted as a "safety valve" for disenchantment. This concept would be challenged by Mikhail Gorbachev's campaign against alcoholism in the 1980s.[32]

The other main criticism of Brezhnev was the post-détente foreign policy,[33] which has been described as imperial overreach or overstretch.[34] Historians such as Paul Kennedy have outlined how they believe empires have traditionally acted beyond their means as they begin to crumble from the inside. Others have consistently shown how politicians have increased their foreign policy activity to distract from a failing domestic agenda.

Brezhnev himself did not have to satisfy an electorate, and his regime had behaved in a restrained and conservative fashion for most of the time it had been in power. Nevertheless, Brezhnev's foreign policy took on a new dimension at the end of the détente years that does fit in with the imperial overstretch thesis. Possibly because the United States was laid low after the catastrophe of the Vietnam War and the shambles of the Watergate Scandal, Washington had

---

[28] Mark Gilbert, *Cold War Europe: The Politics of a Contested Continent* (Rowman & Littlefield, 2014), p. 142.

[29] Edwin Bacon & Mark Sandle, *Brezhnev Reconsidered* (Palgrave Macmillan, 2002), p. 40.

[30] Jason Sharman, *Repression and Resistance in Communist Europe* (Routledge, 2003), p. 23.

[31] Vladislav M. Zubok, *Failed Empire: The Soviet Union in the Cold War from Stalin to Gorbachev* (The University of North Carolina Press, 2007), p. 280.

[32] Stan Fedun, 'How Alcohol Conquered Russia', *The Atlantic*, 25 September 2003, https://www.theatlantic.com/international/archive/2013/09/how-alcohol-conquered-russia/279965/, [accessed 15 May 2019]

[33] Vladislav M. Zubok, *Failed Empire: The Soviet Union in the Cold War from Stalin to Gorbachev* (The University of North Carolina Press, 2007), p.228.

[34] Paul Kennedy, *The Rise and Fall of the Great Powers: Economic Change and Military Conflict from 1500 to 2000* (Random House, 1987).

taken its eye off the foreign policy agenda. It certainly had no appetite for more military adventures. It may have been that the Soviets thought they had the upper hand in the Cold War and that détente had allowed them the breathing space they needed before opening new fronts. Whatever the reasons, Brezhnev launched a number of foreign policy initiatives in the 1970s that would change the calculus of the Cold War itself and ultimately drag the Soviet Union into its own quagmire.

In the mid-1970s, the Soviets engaged in their own version of foreign policy adventurism. This initially manifested itself in Africa, where proxy conflicts still raged. The catalyst for a new round of independence movements and the power struggle associated around these was the colonization of Portugal's overseas territories of Angola and Mozambique. In a similar pattern to other post-colonial African countries such as the Congo, different armed factions competed for power and sought the support of either the United States or the Soviet Union, or sometimes a variant. The Angolan Civil War was fought between three main parties, also drawing in South African irregulars. On the communist side, Fidel Castro's Cuba was most enthusiastic in its support for the left-wing faction, the MPLA (People's Movement for the Liberation of Angola), but the Soviets also supplied it with assistance, including advisors.

A conflict also erupted between Somalia and Ethiopia over a contested border territory in 1977. Having initially backed both sides, Moscow was left with a more straightforward proposition when Somalia attempted to seek other supporters, at which point the Soviets more wholeheartedly got behind Ethiopia which then drove out the Somali troops.

In Mozambique, a civil war started in 1977 when the left-wing FRELIMO (Front for the Liberation of Mozambique) was challenged by the South Africa-backed RENAMO (Mozambican National Resistance) forces. Again, the Soviets backed the left-wing faction (in this case the actual government) with equipment and training.

All this involvement in Africa gravely concerned the United States and fed into the feeling that they had been double-crossed by the Brezhnev regime during détente, but the relationship between Moscow and Washington truly broke down after the Soviets invaded Afghanistan in 1979.

By the late 1970s, Brezhnev was in poor health.[35] A heavy smoker and drinker, Brezhnev had by all accounts increased his alcohol intake in the 1970s and simultaneously began to suffer a series of serious medical issues, most notably heart and respiratory problems. He suffered his first heart attack in 1975 and also experienced strokes.

What is perhaps most surprising was that he was allowed to continue as leader while having such serious health difficulties. It has been suggested that the Soviet leadership was concerned

---

[35] William J. Tompson, *The Soviet Union under Brezhnev*, (Routledge, 2014), p. 180.

that Brezhnev's resignation would stimulate a power struggle and even social unrest. Most transfers of power within the Soviet system had led to some degree of social upheaval, either within the USSR or in its satellite states, or both.

This begs the question of who was making the decisions at the top of the Party in the late 1970s and early 1980s. It seems that a consensus was often found in a Politburo packed with long-term Soviet communists who viewed the world in similar ways, such as Yuri Andropov, Mikhail Suslov, Andrei Gromyko, and Dmitry Ustinov. Historians such as Vladislav Zubok have posited that these Soviet leaders viewed détente a consequence of Soviet military strength, allowing the superpower to flex its military muscles.[36]

However it happened, one of the regime's most fateful decisions was the invasion of Afghanistan, which started on December 26, 1979 when most Western officials were on their Christmas breaks. Afghanistan had long been the scourge of much larger powers attempting to dominate the territory, continuing up until the present day. During the Cold War, the country bordered the Soviet Union republics of Uzbekistan, Tajikistan and Turkmenistan, and Moscow therefore came to believe that securing a communist regime in this border country was in its vital national interests. In April 1978, a communist revolution occurred in Afghanistan, an extremely poor state, bringing to power Nur Muhammad Taraki. This was met with resistance from religious conservatives and an early version of the Islamic mujahideen fighters. The situation was chaotic and highly unstable, and there were threats of coups and countercoups while Taraki and his Foreign Minister Hafizullah Amin committed tens of thousands of murders as the regime attempted to consolidate power. In September 1979, Amin himself overthrew Taraki and had him arrested and murdered.

Brezhnev was concerned about the chain of events in the country and had not supported Amin's coup. With the country descending into anarchy, the Soviets intervened to remove Amin, who they replaced with Babrak Karmal, and sent in a small force to pacify the anti-government agitation, securing a communist Afghanistan. There is some evidence to suggest that Brezhnev himself was opposed to the invasion and was still attached to the idea of détente.[37] Indeed, the two superpowers were due to sign another SALT agreement, but this was ultimately never ratified by Congress, which grew hostile over any further rapprochement with untrustworthy adversaries.

If Brezhnev initially opposed the intervention, he was apparently persuaded by his more hawkish colleagues, namely Andropov, Suslov, and Ustinov,[38] who suggested if the USSR "lost" Afghanistan, the Americans could use it in the same way they exploited Cuba for strategic

---

[36] Vladislav M. Zubok, *Failed Empire: The Soviet Union in the Cold War from Stalin to Gorbachev* (The University of North Carolina Press, 2007), p.259.

[37] Vladislav M. Zubok, *Failed Empire: The Soviet Union in the Cold War from Stalin to Gorbachev* (The University of North Carolina Press, 2007), p.261.

[38] William J. Tompson, *The Soviet Union under Brezhnev*, (Routledge, 2014), p. 29.

reasons.[39] NATO's decision at the same time to deploy new Pershing missiles in West Germany may have also hardened attitudes in Moscow.[40]

When Soviet tanks rolled into Afghanistan on December 26, 1979, it caused outrage across the Western world, but the Red Army's "short" intervention would last almost 10 years and lead to the deaths of almost 15,000 Soviet soldiers, tens of thousands of Afghan fighters, and maybe up to two million Afghan civilians. It proved to be just as unwinnable as America's calamitous intervention in Vietnam.[41]

The Brezhnev regime experienced increasing international condemnation in the late 1970s, and its stance on human rights drew many opponents. Brezhnev would serve as leader of the Soviet Union until his death at the end of 1982, and during these final years, the relationship between the superpowers declined.

The first obvious demonstration of this was at the 1980 Summer Winter Olympic Games. Having been granted the games back in 1974, the Soviets did what every country hosting a major sporting event does: attempt to use them to bolster their international image. For the USSR, this meant a tidal wave of propaganda, demonstrating to the world the apparent superiority of the Soviet model. Unfortunately for Brezhnev, the Olympics were boycotted by the United States and 65 other countries due to its invasion of Afghanistan. The other countries boycotting the games were mainly U.S. allies in Latin America, Asia, and Africa, but China also boycotted. For Brezhnev, the boycott was a humiliation.

Foreign policy was also becoming a nightmare for the Brezhnev regime. More trouble brewed in Eastern Europe, this time in Poland. The Poles had protested in the mid-1950s and early 1970s over issues ranging from food prices to political accountability, and in addition to exhibiting growing nationalist tendencies, they also retained a deep religious faith. The role of Pope John Paul II, a Pole, would play a part in undermining communist rule in the country.

In 1980, however, it was workers' demands in the port of Gdansk that drove protests around the country and the foundation of the first trade union unaffiliated with the state, *Solidarity*, led by Lech Walesa. The crisis led to a change in leadership within the Polish Communist Party, and the demonstrations dragged on well into 1981.

The Brezhnev regime was becoming increasingly animated about the situation, concerned that the West would try and prise the Poles out of the Soviet sphere of influence. To be fair, the concern was justified because the British, French, and Americans were working behind the

---

[39] Vladislav M. Zubok, *Failed Empire: The Soviet Union in the Cold War from Stalin to Gorbachev* (The University of North Carolina Press, 2007), p.263.
[40] Vladislav M. Zubok, *Failed Empire: The Soviet Union in the Cold War from Stalin to Gorbachev* (The University of North Carolina Press, 2007), p.253.
[41] William J. Tompson, *The Soviet Union under Brezhnev*, (Routledge, 2014), p. 112.

scenes to encourage liberal reform in Poland. Nevertheless, Brezhnev made it clear to Warsaw that if it did not tamp down the protests, the Soviets would be forced to intervene, much the way they had in Czechoslovakia in 1968.[42] The Brezhnev Doctrine was still alive and well.[43]

Ultimately, Polish General Wojciech Jaruzelski took power within the country's Politburo and initiated martial law and a crackdown against dissents. Protests would again occur towards the end of the decade, this time drawing concessions from the communist authorities and ultimately leading to elections and a transition to democracy. For all of Brezhnev's hard power, it was not enough to truly subdue the peoples of Central and Eastern Europe.

Throughout this time, the war in Afghanistan continued to rage, and the conflict had taken on a clear ideological dividing line. On one side were the communists, supported by the Soviets and nominally atheist, and on the other were the mujahideen. The war attracted fighters from across the Islamic world, including hardliners that would form the core of some of the world's most notorious terrorist groups in the 1990s and 2000s. At this point, however, the Americans were happy to support these religious warriors against a common foe. The U.S. started to funnel weapons to the militias through Pakistan, while the Soviets committed more and more troops and materiel, with ever decreasing results.

In many respects, the Afghanistan War was a mirror of the American involvement in Vietnam. The domestic population became increasingly unhappy over the deaths of their fathers, sons, brothers, and husbands for an apparently futile cause, and it increasingly damaged the superpower's prestige. As the Brezhnev regime became increasingly sucked into the Afghan theater, the Carter administration, which was focused on human rights and the ethical dimensions of the Cold War, was replaced by the ardent anti-communist Reagan administration. Along with Britain's Margaret Thatcher, Reagan was an aggressive critic of the USSR's actions, and he extended Carter's ideological criticism of the communist system, famously describing the Soviet Union as an "Evil Empire" shortly after Brezhnev's death.[44]

Whereas earlier in his tenure, Brezhnev could make some claim to the moral high ground, by the early 1980s his regime was under siege by critics attempting to undermine his country's ideological foundations. Matters were not helped by Brezhnev's poor health, which deteriorated further in 1981 and allowed a collection of hardliners to make key decisions. Andropov, Suslov, Gromyko, and Ustinov further damaged Moscow's international prestige.

The one development that warranted optimism was the thawing of relations between the Soviet

---

[42] Godfrey Hodgson, *People's Century: From the dawn of the century to the eve of the millennium* (Godalming: BBC Books, 1998)

[43] Matthew J. Ouimet, *Rise and Fall of the Brezhnev Doctrine in Soviet Foreign Policy*, (The University of North Carolina Press, 2003), p. 131.

[44] Godfrey Hodgson, *People's Century: From the dawn of the century to the eve of the millennium* (Godalming: BBC Books, 1998)

Union and China. After Mao's death in 1976, a power struggle had unfolded, eventually leaving reformer Deng Xiaoping in charge. Deng was far more pragmatic than Mao and primarily focused on improving the Chinese economy while improving relations with neighbors.

During Brezhnev's final years, the economy continued to slump. In terms of GDP, the Soviet economy continued to grow, but the expansion of 1-2% was far too low for a developing country such as the USSR. The Soviets would spend much of the 1980s attempting to reduce spending and increase economic output, but Brezhnev and his advisors were wholly unqualified to accomplish that, and they repeatedly failed to significantly improve living conditions.

Although the Soviet Union had done its best to insulate it from the global capitalist economy, in the early 1980s this was becoming difficult. Interest rates had been hiked by the U.S. Federal Reserve in an attempt to squeeze inflation out of its own economy, and with falling commodity prices, these trends damaged a number of governments, in particular communist allies of the Soviet Union. The situation would grow even more desperate as the decade progressed, and even as the Soviet economy remained sclerotic, the Politburo was overly reluctant to implement reforms.

Brezhnev and his colleagues were also resistant to any criticism regarding human rights. It continued to impede the emigration of Soviet Jews and fill jails with political prisoners. Rather than the Stalin-era network of Gulag prisons, separate towns were established to keep and seal off troublesome citizens, such as "PERM-36," to the North East of Moscow.[45] It was in this kind of setting that Andrei Sakharov continued to be held until his release in 1986. Sakharov was famous across the world, and his persistent hunger strikes threatened to further embarrass the Soviet regime.

Brezhnev did not wield power in 1982 despite remaining in office. He rarely appeared in public and had another serious stroke that May. By the time he died on November 10, 1982, other members of the Politburo had been vying for the top position as it became clear that Brezhnev was close to death.

Gorbachev's Immediate Challenges

Mikhail Suslov, who was already 79 himself, had been assumed to be one of the favorites, but he died in January 1982, paving the way for Yuri Andropov. As the former head of the KGB, Andropov was obviously connected with the levers of power within the Soviet Union, so it was perhaps unsurprising that he assumed power in a relatively straightforward fashion shortly after Brezhnev's death. To the outside world, Andropov looked like he would pursue a tougher line than Brezhnev, but in reality he had already been crucial in making decisions the past few years,

---

[45] BBC Radio 4, 'I was imprisoned in Stalin's Gulag', *Witness*, 9 September 2015, https://www.bbc.com/news/av/magazine-34155914/i-was-imprisoned-in-stalin-s-gulag, [accessed 4 December 2018]

so there was plenty of continuity.

Andropov

Andropov was 68 when he took office, and while that was relatively young for a member of the Soviet Politburo, he died on February 9, 1984 of kidney failure. He was replaced by an even older man, Konstantin Chernenko, who was 72 and ill when he came to power. He died as a result of respiratory, heart, and liver problems on March 10, 1985. Mikhail Gorbachev took power in the Soviet Union a day later, at the age of 54.

Gorbachev

As with most communist leaders during the era, little was known about the individual preferences of each member of the Politburo. From the outside, Gorbachev appeared to be an orthodox communist likely to continue the policies of his predecessor. Born in 1931 in the Stavropol Krai region of Russia, located in the North Caucasus, Gorbachev had been a dutiful communist. Rising through the ranks of the regional party, he became head of the Stavropol region in 1970 and a member of the key Central Committee of the Soviet Union the following year. This marked Gorbachev's entry onto the national stage, and in 1980, he became a full member of the inner circle, the Politburo. Intriguingly,

Gorbachev's closest ally on the Politburo was Yuri Andropov, the former head of the KGB and seemingly hard-line, orthodox communist. It may be a sign of Gorbachev's political cunning that he garnered Andropov's support, or simply that he exhibited few signs of the reforming zeal that would so mark him out as different to his colleagues after he became party General Secretary in 1985.

Indeed, Gorbachev was Andropov's favored successor, as the aging leader considered the younger man capable of breaking out of the cycle of geriatric leaders that characterized this period of Soviet politics. When Andropov died in 1984, however, the compromise candidate was the frail Konstantin Chernenko, who was actually older than Andropov. It would not be until Chernenko's death that Gorbachev actually took power.

Perhaps the only exception to the belief that Gorbachev showed no pedigree of reform came in 1984 when he met British Prime Minister Margaret Thatcher. The meeting was judged subsequently to be a sign that if Gorbachev became a future Soviet leader, the relationship between the West and the communist world could potentially improve markedly. Thatcher had been described by the Soviet leadership as an "Iron Lady" before she became Prime Minister, a sobriquet she liked so much she encouraged its use, and by 1984 she had established herself as a foreign policy hawk, particularly after the 1982 Falklands War. Nevertheless, Thatcher had been infuriated by the Soviet leadership, mostly due their stilted and unimaginative manner, and inflexibility regarding policy.

In December 1984, just months before he was given the opportunity to lead the Soviet Union, Mikhail Gorbachev visited Thatcher in Britain. He was invited to the Prime Minister's countryside retreat, *Chequers*, for wide-ranging discussions on foreign policy, nuclear weapons, the geopolitical situation in Eastern Europe, and more.[46] Thatcher was surprized by Gorbachev's openness and immediately recognized that he was a different kind of Soviet leader,[47] famously declaring, "I like Mr Gorbachev. We can do business together." The timing of the meeting was serendipitous for the Gorbachev-Thatcher relationship. The next time they met was at the funeral of Konstantin Chernenko in March 1985 as Gorbachev prepared to take power.[48]

What had been clear to Thatcher in 1984 was that Gorbachev was animated about the Strategic Defense Initiative (SDI) and seemed ready to pre-negotiate other arms limitation talks, including offensive weapons, in return for concessions on SDI.[49] The project was widely derided and jokingly referred to as "Star Wars," costing hundreds of billions and never getting anywhere near implementation. In terms of Cold War strategy, however, SDI worked perfectly, and the Soviets took the threat of SDI at face value. If Star Wars became operational, it would render the Soviet nuclear arsenal redundant against the United States. Western Europe would then be the Soviets' target, which is why SDI concerned both the Soviet bloc and American allies in Europe, especially Thatcher. In terms of treaty obligations, SDI also effectively breached the terms of the ABM (Anti-Ballistic Missile) agreement, made between the US and Soviets in 1968. The idea of ABM was to set a level playing field and curb the arms race.

---

[46] John Campbell, *Margaret Thatcher Volume Two: The Iron Lady* (Random House, 2003), pp. 285-286.
[47] Margaret Thatcher, *The Downing Street Years* (Harper Collins, 1993), pp. 459-463.
[48] John Campbell, *Margaret Thatcher Volume Two: The Iron Lady* (Random House, 2003), p. 286.
[49] Charles Moore, *Margaret Thatcher The Authorized Biography: Volume Two Everything She Wants* (Allen Lane, 2015), pp. 232-233.

In December 1984, neither Thatcher nor Gorbachev were in positions to negotiate with each other, but nevertheless the message was relayed to the Reagan administration that Gorbachev would be a useful contact for better relations between the West and Moscow. Little did they know that they would get the chance to deal with Gorbachev, this time in a position of ultimate responsibility, much quicker than anticipated.

Despite the signs of an opening between Gorbachev and Britain, the situation he inherited in March 1985 was challenging to say the least. The Soviets had escalated the Cold War in the late 1970s by stepping up its support for left wing movements and governments in Africa and Central America, and the Americans had elected the anti-communist Ronald Reagan in November 1980. It wasn't long before President Reagan called the Soviet Union an "evil empire," and he would famously demand that Gorbachev tear down the Berlin Wall.

Reagan and Gorbachev in 1986

With positions toughening on both sides, superpower tension increased in the early 1980s, and the arms race seemed to be back after a period of détente in the early 1970s. It was during this period that an escalation of the Cold War seemed possible, either by design or through a miscalculation. An example of the former was the deployment of the new Pershing nuclear weapons by NATO into West Germany despite vigorous dissent among Western domestic populations. In 1983, a NATO exercise, Operation Able Archer, triggered panic on the Soviet side and came alarmingly close to a nuclear escalation. Moreover, the Soviets shot down a civilian plane, South Korean Air flight KAL007, in August 1983 which led to increased hostility, threats, and counterthreats on both sides.

The United States hosted the 1984 Olympic Games in Los Angeles, and the event was boycotted by the Soviets in retaliation for the American boycott of the 1980 games in Moscow. The West constantly criticized the Soviet war in Afghanistan and offered material support to the anti-Soviet Islamic militias known as the Mujahideen. The Soviets meanwhile lambasted the Reagan administration for its wholehearted support of right-wing forces in Latin America, many of which committed grave human rights violations, such as in El Salvador and Nicaragua.

The Soviet regime that Gorbachev inherited believed that Star Wars would give the United States overwhelming military superiority, and many of Gorbachev's subsequent decisions were based upon the premise that the Soviet Union needed to make an accommodation with the US on nuclear weapons or reestablish the principles of the ABM and other arms limitation agreements, such as SALT (Strategic Arms Limitation Talks). What made this even more urgent was that Gorbachev clearly understood that the USSR could not afford to match the US on arms, even in the unlikely event that it could develop technology like SDI. The true strength of the Soviets during the Cold War was in the intelligence sphere, but this was unlikely to provide the resources to match such an undertaking as SDI. Indeed, part of Gorbachev's strategy was to reduce the spending commitments that the Soviets had built up during the Cold War.

Furthermore, Gorbachev was also faced with the war in Afghanistan. Having invaded the country at the end of 1979 as a means of propping up a communist regime in Kabul, the Soviet army and air force had become bogged down in guerrilla warfare. There was little attachment from the Afghan population towards communism, and the main opposition formed around religious groups and militias. These mujahideen were increasingly supported by US hardware, most infamously surface to air missiles, so-called "stingers" which began to terrorize Soviet planes and helicopters. Gorbachev had always been skeptical of the war despite the fact Andropov was one of its architects. With the Soviets in an Afghan quagmire by 1985, Gorbachev would also quickly seek to extricate his country from the conflict.

Gorbachev's Tentative Domestic Reforms

Gorbachev came to power as a slow economic and political crisis gripped the Soviet Union, though this was not immediately obvious to outside observers. After all, the communist system intended to iron out the boom and bust tendencies of a market economy, and provide consistent, centrally-planned growth and increasing living standards. However, bubbling under the surface were serious problems, and Gorbachev moved quickly to denounce the approach of his predecessors - who were conveniently no longer alive - as flawed. In particular he vilified the Brezhnev era as one of corruption and stagnation, and indeed, the Soviet economy had become sclerotic by the mid-1980s, devoid of momentum, dynamism and new ideas.[50]

What made things particularly acute was that the United States had managed to apply enough pressure on oil-producing countries like Saudi Arabia for the oil price to fall. Oil prices had been particularly damaging to the West during the 1970s as the OPEC cartel increased prices following the 1973 Arab-Israeli War, then the 1979 Iranian Revolution. In the 1980s, lower prices had the opposite effect, starving the oil-producing USSR of vital hard currency. The limited economic data available on the Soviet Union showed how its economy slowed in the late 1970s, and did not recover for the rest of its existence.[51] In addition, although industrialized, the Soviet Union still had the hallmarks of a developing economy and therefore required much higher rates of growth to improve its population's standard of living. This was the economic situation that Gorbachev inherited in March 1985.

Gorbachev was a more imaginative leader than his predecessors. Whereas most other Soviet leaders would have been guided by events, particularly in the economic sphere, Gorbachev had already worked out his own theory of his country's ailments. To summarize, his analysis shared much with the "Prague Spring" of late 1960s Czechoslovakia, where communist leader Alexander Dubček had outlined a reform project known as "socialism with a human face." Gorbachev's version of these principles drew on similar themes: socialism in and of itself was a virtuous system, but it needed improving. The way to do this was to unleash the energy of its citizens by loosening political constraints. Therefore, Gorbachev sought to reduce the omnipotent fear of dissent in the mid-1980s and unleash a wave of creative power that would drive the country's economy and increase growth, living standards, and the USSR's position relative to the United States. The new Soviet leader still believed that Soviet communism was a superior system to Western liberal capitalism, and that it simply needed reform.[52]

The sequencing of his programme was crucial. Political liberalization would come first, which would lead to economic results. It was the polar opposite to what was already underway in Deng Xiaoping's communist China. which focused on economic liberalization while maintaining

[50] Mark Gilbert, *Cold War Europe: The Politics of a Contested Continent* (Rowman & Littlefield, 2014), p. 142.
[51] Edwin Bacon & Mark Sandle, *Brezhnev Reconsidered* (Palgrave Macmillan, 2002), p. 40.
[52] CNN, *Cold War* (TV Series, produced by Jeremy Isaacs and Pat Mitchell, 1998)

political strictures.

In his first months in office, Gorbachev showed glimpses of the road he wanted to take. He traveled around the USSR, often stopping to speak to ordinary people on the street, encouraging them to speak their minds. The Soviet leader also discouraged portraits of him, hoping to avoid the kind of cult of personality of previous leaders that Gorbachev believed to be inane. He also packed the Politburo with reformers and supporters, knowing that the changes he planned to enact would likely lead to resistance from orthodox hardliners. He made the veteran foreign minister Andrei Gromyko head of state, replaced him with reformer Eduard Shevardnadze, and brought key allies Alexander Yakovlev and Anatoly Lukyanov into the Politburo.

Yakovlev

Shevardnadze

Gorbachev's first big idea in domestic affairs was *Perestroika,* or restructuring, and targeted work practices and economic policy. The Soviet leader had identified the inefficient approach to production as a key impediment to better economic performance. Gorbachev was desperate to find a way to improve the productivity of the Soviet economy, without actually transforming it into a market system. His Perestroika programme intended to improve the communist system. At its core, however, Perestroika was vague and nebulous. As historian Vladislav Zubok has noted, Perestroika "eluded definition and systemization."[53] The forces it set free, along with later political liberalising, set the country on a path to tumult, including within the Politburo.[54] The

---

[53] Vladislav M. Zubok*, Failed Empire: The Soviet Union in the Cold War from Stalin to Gorbachev* (The University of North Carolina Press, 2007), p. 279.
[54] Michael McFaul, *Russia's Unfinished Revolution: Political Change from Gorbachev to Putin* (Cornell University Press, 2002), p. 78.

obstacles to economic reform were huge.[55] With towns and cities effectively monopsonies, that is to say there was often one major employer or factory, there was no competition and few incentives for Soviets to increase productivity. Although in the past communist regimes had set ludicrous production targets, these were treated with great scepticism, if not derision, by the 1980s. Without private property, central planners also found it hard to encourage greater efficiency or generate energy around reform.

Gorbachev launched his Perestroika agenda in a speech in May 1985 and, unusually for a communist leader, took the opportunity to criticize the regime's economic policies. That said, there was little concrete action for the first two years of Perestroika, save for encouragement from the top to improve efficiency and productivity. The Gorbachev regime thought, erroneously, that removing inefficient and corrupt bureaucrats may suffice to encourage better economic performance, marking a cautious start to "modernization."[56]

More substantial changes came after the 27th Congress of the Soviet Communist Party in 1987, but Gorbachev's failure to fundamentally revive the Soviet economy was one of the crucial reasons he oversaw the eventual collapse of the USSR. A related factor was political reform, which gave Soviet citizens the opportunity to air their pent-up grievances, as well as provide oxygen to ideas antithetical to the Soviet model, such as nationalism. Gorbachev, however, appeared to have much greater success with this programme in his first two years in office, the name of which became recognizable around the world: *Glasnost*. Meaning "openness and transparency," Gorbachev adopted the term as a slogan in June 1986. Glasnost was a relaxation of censorship, even encouraging - at least by Soviet standards - freedom of expression. This was initially focused on art and literature and gave unprecedented freedom to publishers.[57]

Gorbachev delegated the programme to his ally, Alexander Yakovlev, who set in motion a series of astonishingly liberal measures.[58] Yakovlev encouraged the setting up of reformist publications and then installed liberal editors. These titles, such as *Moscow News* and *Ogonek* discussed previously unheard-of taboos in the cultural, economic and political spheres. Suddenly Soviet history was open to discussion and debate. After almost 70 years of suffocating political repression, Glasnost was like a breath of fresh air, one that many Soviet citizens were unprepared for. Gorbachev passed laws in 1987 that provided further freedom of expression and association.[59] In 1987 Moscow stopped blocking the signals of Western radio stations such as Germany's *Deutsche Welle*, the US's *Voice of America* and Britain's *BBC*.[60] After Perestroika, the Glasnost

[55] Archie Brown, *The Gorbachev Factor* (Oxford University Press, 1996), p. 136.
[56] Vladislav M. Zubok, *Failed Empire: The Soviet Union in the Cold War from Stalin to Gorbachev* (The University of North Carolina Press, 2007), p. 279.
[57] Michael McFaul, *Russia's Unfinished Revolution: Political Change from Gorbachev to Putin* (Cornell University Press, 2002), p. 64.
[58] Michael McFaul, *Russia's Unfinished Revolution: Political Change from Gorbachev to Putin* (Cornell University Press, 2002), p. 64.
[59] Michael McFaul, *Russia's Unfinished Revolution: Political Change from Gorbachev to Putin* (Cornell University Press, 2002), p. 64.

liberalisation agenda garnered further enemies in the Soviet corridors of power.

A well-known early beneficiary of Gorbachev's new agenda was Andrei Sakharov. One of the communist world's most famous political prisoners, Sakharov was a Soviet nuclear scientist who had begun criticizing the regime in the 1960s, invoking human rights over the following decade. A thorn in the side of the Brezhnev government, Sakharov was jailed after his participation in protests against the invasion of Afghanistan in 1979. Isolated in Gorky, Sakharov had engaged in hunger strikes and was an intermittent embarrassment for the Soviet regime, which was terrified that he would die in jail. One of Sakharov's principle complaints was that the Soviet Union had signed up to the 1975 Helsinki Final Act without implementing any of the treaty's human rights provisions. Gorbachev himself would take these commitments far more seriously and essentially closed the residual elements of the Gulag prison network which had so tainted the reputation of the USSR over the course of its history. In fact, Gorbachev would stay relatively close to Sakharov after his release as the human rights activist took full advantage of Glasnost to pursue a position of unofficial political leadership before becoming a Deputy in the USSR's first ever elections in 1989.

[60] Vladislav M. Zubok, *Failed Empire: The Soviet Union in the Cold War from Stalin to Gorbachev* (The University of North Carolina Press, 2007), p. 298.

Sakharov

One of the rapid byproducts of the Glasnost agenda was a desire by some for more democratic accountability in the USSR. As Michael McFaul has outlined, this allowed Sakharov to become the "moral leader of Russia's emerging democratic opposition."[61] During this heady period, many of Gorbachev's inner circle believed they could ride the tiger of liberalization while continuing the centrally-controlled communist system. The essential contradiction within this point of view would only become obvious later.

Two of the men who turned Gorbachev's agenda into reality were both named Yakovlev, though they were unrelated. Alexander Yakovlev can be thought of as the "chief ideologist" of Perestroika.[62] Technically in charge of propaganda, Alexander Yakovlev effectively turned the Soviet Union into a more normal state, eliminating many of the false statements of past years. Promoted to the Politburo in 1987, he admitted to the Soviet Union's participation in the 1939 Molotov-Ribbentrop Pact, the agreement between Stalin and Hitler that had initially kept the USSR out of the Second World War. This was a highly unusual, but symbolic gesture for a Soviet politician. It also attracted the ire of the hardliners, who made it a priority to oust him, which they duly did after an attack on him at the 28th Congress in July 1990.

Meanwhile, Yegor Yakovlev was responsible for transforming the press environment of the USSR as editor and champion of a more open media setting. Yegor cultivated that most un-Soviet of things, a respected media outlet, with his work on *Moscow News*. Despite not being related, the two Yakovlev's were close and were key to the change in tone in Gorbachev's USSR.[63] Between the pair, amongst others, they helped bring the concept of objective truth closer to the Soviet people, but, as Arkady Ostrovsky has noted, without the official lies of Soviet propaganda, the state lacked legitimacy in many people's eyes.[64]

One of Gorbachev's earliest initiatives was his "war on alcoholism."[65] Launched at the same time as Perestroika in May 1985, most of the Politburo now adopted a curious stance.[66] Soviet leaders had been known for their penchant for drinking alcohol and would continue to be in the future, and Soviet leaders had long tolerated heavy drinking among the wider population as a means of distraction from the often-stultifying conditions of everyday life. This would all change under Gorbachev, who saw chronic alcoholism as another symptom of the malaise of Soviet

---

[61] Michael McFaul, *Russia's Unfinished Revolution: Political Change from Gorbachev to Putin* (Cornell University Press, 2002), p. 65.

[62] Arkady Ostrovsky, *The Invention of Russia: The Journey from Gorbachev's Freedom to Putin's War* (Atlantic Books, 2015), p. 13.

[63] Arkady Ostrovsky, *The Invention of Russia: The Journey from Gorbachev's Freedom to Putin's War* (Atlantic Books, 2015), p. 15.

[64] Arkady Ostrovsky, *The Invention of Russia: The Journey from Gorbachev's Freedom to Putin's War* (Atlantic Books, 2015), p. 15.

[65] Vladislav M. Zubok, *Failed Empire: The Soviet Union in the Cold War from Stalin to Gorbachev* (The University of North Carolina Press, 2007), p. 280.

[66] Archie Brown, *The Gorbachev Factor* (Oxford University Press, 1996), p. 141.

society, namely its poor productivity and general low morale. The anti-alcohol campaign, led by Yegor Ligachev, contained a number of strands, including general anti-alcohol propaganda and specified restrictions in the sale, supply, and distribution of alcohol. The campaign initially gained traction in part because Gorbachev was a light drinker in comparison with his peers. The restrictions on alcohol, however, became increasingly unpopular as the campaign wore on.

One of the most notorious events of the Gorbachev era was the nuclear disaster at the Chernobyl plant in April 1986. Despite his reputation for transparency, Gorbachev's woeful response to the catastrophe demonstrated the limits of his personal influence and capabilities in the USSR at this time. The longer-term problems would only become clear in the years ahead, but in 1986, the Soviet authorities attempted to keep news of the disaster a secret. It was only days after the explosion at the nuclear power plant that the regime admitted something had happened, and this was only after a nuclear power plant in Sweden had detected high levels of radiation. The lackluster response of the Soviet government ensured it was lambasted for incompetence across the world, and it heightened concerns over nuclear power in general, particularly in secretive and deceitful states such as the Soviet Union. Chernobyl is sure to be one of the most enduring aspects of Gorbachev's legacy, as the area is estimated to remain contaminated for decades, if not centuries.[67]

---

[67] Richard Pérez-Peña, "Decades Later and Far Away, Chernobyl Disaster Still Contaminates Milk," *The New York Times*, 8 June 2018, https://www.nytimes.com/2018/06/08/world/europe/chernobyl-nuclear-disaster-radiation-milk.html, [accessed 21 May 2019]

A picture of the damage at Chernobyl after the accident

Gorbachev's Early Foreign Policy

In the mid-1980s, the communist world was in a state of flux. Many of the regimes in the region were wobbling.[68] Poland had only recently ended martial law, and in East Germany the regime was struggling for hard currency. Romania was under the full grip of its megalomaniac leader Nicolae Ceaușescu, who lived in splendor while subjecting his people to misery, living through freezing cold in the winter with little food or consumer goods on the shelves of shops. Hungary was one of the only countries to implement liberalizing economic reform, but Central and Eastern Europe were expected to toe Moscow's line. Whereas previously this might have involved a crackdown on reformists or dissidents, after Gorbachev came to power, the satellite

---

[68] CNN, *Cold War* (TV Series, produced by Jeremy Isaacs and Pat Mitchell, 1998)

states in Europe were now expected to pursue Glasnost and Perestroika. In some respects, Gorbachev actually expected communist leaders in Central and Eastern Europe to think for themselves, which proved to be a tough task. T

he other countries broadly aligned with the Soviet Union also struggled to keep up with Gorbachev's reforms, and nowhere was this as relevant as in communist Yugoslavia. After Tito's death in 1980, Yugoslavia appeared, for all intents and purposes, to be prospering, implementing its more flexible form of communism. Nevertheless, a more open political atmosphere posed serious problems for Belgrade, because if citizens could discuss politics in a more open environment, they could potentially discuss previously forbidden topics such as nationalism. This would prove as fatal for the Soviet Union as it proved later for Yugoslavia, but these issues were largely hidden from view in the first few years of the Gorbachev era.

Despite the increasingly belligerent rhetoric of the early 1980s, the Politburo wanted to return to détente.[69] In geopolitics, it is often easier for hardliners to make agreements with apparently sworn enemies. Reagan presented a much tougher foreign policy to the world, rhetorically lambasting the entire communist system and philosophy, offering material support for anti-communist forces in Central America, and deploying nuclear weapons in Western Europe to oppose the Soviet missiles there. He was a consistent critic of the Soviet involvement in Afghanistan and encouraged the CIA to provide aid to the anti-Soviet militias in that theatre. In short, Moscow saw Reagan as a potentially dangerous opponent who had raised the stakes in the Cold War, so Gorbachev's administration wanted to reduce Cold War tension and return to 1970s-style détente.

Ultimately, Reagan and Gorbachev developed a dialogue, assisted by intermediaries such as Thatcher and Canadian Prime Minister Pierre Trudeau, and they subsequently met at a serious of superpower summits. The SDI was the issue that urgently brought Gorbachev to the negotiating table. Foreign policy was tightly controlled by Gorbachev and his foreign minister, Eduard Shevardnadze, who had no previous experience in foreign affairs but did enjoy the confidence of the General Secretary.[70] Gorbachev and Shevardnadze pressed the Americans for a face-to-face meeting, seeking a commitment to reduce the number of offensive weapons and persuade Reagan to shelve the Star Wars project. Essentially, Gorbachev wanted a reversion to a 1972 version of détente in which both offensive and defensive weapons would be controlled and limited.

As it turned out, Reagan was actually a proponent of nuclear disarmament, a fact that only became clear as his second term progressed. The American president was actually open to any Soviet overture that involved reducing or removing the threat of nuclear weapons. Deterrence

---

[69] Vladislav M. Zubok, *Failed Empire: The Soviet Union in the Cold War from Stalin to Gorbachev* (The University of North Carolina Press, 2007), p. 280.
[70] Vladislav M. Zubok, *Failed Empire: The Soviet Union in the Cold War from Stalin to Gorbachev* (The University of North Carolina Press, 2007), p. 280.

had been the principle that had led to the arms race and then détente in the Cold War, yet Reagan thought deterrence was wrongheaded.[71] It would bring Reagan into a fierce dispute with other Western leaders such as Thatcher, as well as the hardliners in his own administration. Nevertheless, it was Thatcher who broke the logjam for a Reagan-Gorbachev meeting. By publicly endorsing Gorbachev and claiming he was someone with whom she could "do business," she had paved the way for a meeting with Reagan.

The first meeting between Reagan and Gorbachev came on November 19-20, 1985 in Geneva, but the signs had not been promising leading up to the summit. The Americans dismissed out of hand any concessions over Star Wars, and a reduction in offensive warheads also seemed out of reach. The meeting, however, yielded some results insofar as the two leaders showed some warmth towards each other. Meeting in private there appeared little common ground and few points of agreement between the pair, but they were both optimistic politicians and developed a rapport. At the time, Reagan's aides and some of the Western press were concerned that the American would be bamboozled by the younger, perhaps wily Soviet leader, and indeed, despite the personal bond, Gorbachev was dismissive of Reagan's political views, famously telling his colleagues he considered the president a "troglodyte."[72]

Although a dialogue had opened between Reagan and Gorbachev, which was more than could be said for the previous six years, the two leaders left Geneva without any firm agreement or statement of aims. In and of itself, the summit seemed to be a disappointment, but now it is looked upon as the first step in a new stage of détente which led to a much greater understanding between the superpowers.

The next summit, at Reykjavik, would be more dramatic. Held almost a year after Geneva, on October 11-12, 1986, Reagan and Gorbachev met once again in the Icelandic capital. The summit had actually been postponed on several occasions, with tensions remaining high between the superpowers despite the warmer relationship of the two leaders at Geneva. Finally, a meeting was set and the pair met at another chilly location in a relatively neutral country. This time the conversations moved into a much deeper and serious direction. Reagan expressed his dislike of nuclear weapons, wanting to see them eradicated altogether and linking that belief to his SDI project. At this stage, Gorbachev did seem to outwit the older man, proposing that both sides decommission all nuclear weapons within 10 years, the so-called "zero option."[73] Shocked, Reagan agreed that this was in fact a good idea, one that he could support.

The proposal to completely remove all nuclear weapons disturbed advisors on both sides, and a counterproposal was agreed that would eliminate all but 100 nuclear weapons on each side. The

---

[71] CNN, *Cold War* (TV Series, produced by Jeremy Isaacs and Pat Mitchell, 1998)

[72] William Taubman, *Gorbachev: His Life and Times*. New York City: Simon and Schuster, 2017), p. 304.

[73] Tom Wicker, "The Zero Option Revived," *The New York Times*, 4 March 1987, https://www.nytimes.com/1987/03/04/opinion/in-the-nation-the-zero-option-revived.html, [accessed 22 May 2019]

idea received the support of Secretary of State George Shultz, and the summit appeared to be heading for a historic conclusion until Gorbachev pursued the SDI issue as a prerequisite of any agreement. Differences then emerged, and Reagan introduced a number of the West's criticisms of the Soviet Union since the previous period of détente, including human rights, the right of Soviet Jews to emigrate, and the war in Afghanistan. Gorbachev wanted SDI to be shelved, a condition Reagan would not countenance. As a result, the talks broke down and Reagan and Gorbachev left Reykjavik without a deal. More progress had been made for sure, but anything more concrete was proving elusive.[74] The Soviets were initially disappointed at the outcome of Reykjavik, but Gorbachev and Shevardnadze soon realized that they were on the cusp of something substantial if they could find a way through the obstacles on view at Reykjavik.

Shultz

The fallout for Reagan appeared to be more challenging than for Gorbachev. A furious Margaret Thatcher flew almost straightaway to Camp David, the presidential retreat, to berate Reagan over his proposed stance on nuclear disarmament. Thatcher was committed to the longstanding policy of nuclear deterrence and was disturbed that Reagan had been apparently

---

[74] CNN, *Cold War* (TV Series, produced by Jeremy Isaacs and Pat Mitchell, 1998)

close to ditching the core strategy of the Western alliance.

A month later, Reagan faced the biggest crisis of his Presidency: Iran Contra. In November 1986, it emerged that the US had secretly sold weapons to Iran - then a mortal American foe - and used the proceeds to fund the anti-communist forces in Nicaragua, where Congress had prohibited military support. Reagan survived the scandal, but it dogged him for the rest of his term.

Meanwhile, Gorbachev was visited in March 1987 by Thatcher, who was received warmly both by the Soviet leader and the crowds. Very unusually for a communist regime, Thatcher was allowed to participate in a television debate, during which she made the case for the superiority of the capitalist, democratic system. She also visited a church at a time when organized religion was not encouraged in the Soviet Union, and she had an open discussion with Gorbachev himself. Thatcher questioned the plan that had been tabled at Reykjavik on nuclear disarmament, saying that this would simply see a return of conventional warfare. As was her way during this period of the Cold War, she also met with well-known dissidents such as Sakharov.[75]

As had been the case at their 1984 meeting in Britain, the two leaders debated matters in a robust and - according to Thatcher's official biographer Charles Moore - even rude fashion.[76] Nevertheless, it appears that Gorbachev had no qualms rigorously arguing with Western world leaders and ending these conversations with his respect for his opponent heightened. It was a highly unusual visit and further evidence that the Soviet Union was changing rapidly.

It was perhaps surprising that Thatcher and Gorbachev developed such a good relationship given some of the events taking place behind the scenes. The streets and backstreets of Europe had long been the setting for espionage in the Cold War, and in the early years of the conflict it seemed that the best-known "double agents" worked for Moscow. However, the opposite trend emerged in the 1980s, and one of the biggest spy coups during this period was the identification of Oleg Gordievsky as a double agent working for Britain. Having joined the KGB in 1963 at the age of 25, Gordievsky, who became disenchanted with his country after the 1968 invasion of Czechoslovakia, was turned in the mid-1970s and provided intelligence to the British for a full 10 years.[77] Indeed, it was Gordievsky's intelligence that helped defuse the 1983 crisis over Operation Able Archer. At the time working in London, Gordievsky was essentially discovered by the KGB in May 1985, just after Gorbachev had become General Secretary, and recalled to Moscow for interrogation.[78] The British and Gordievsky hatched an escape plan and, astonishingly, managed to spirit the spy across the Finnish border, flying him to Britain on July

[75] Margaret Thatcher, *The Downing Street Years* (Harper Collins, 1993), p. 481.

[76] Charles Moore, *Margaret Thatcher The Authorized Biography: Volume Two Everything She Wants* (Allen Lane, 2015), p. 623.

[77] Charles Moore, *Margaret Thatcher The Authorized Biography: Volume Two Everything She Wants* (Allen Lane, 2015), p. 115.

[78] Charles Moore, *Margaret Thatcher The Authorized Biography: Volume Two Everything She Wants* (Allen Lane, 2015), p. 263.

22, 1985.[79]

The British kept the news of Gordievsky's defection quiet for several weeks - the Soviets believed Gordievsky had committed suicide - until late August, when Thatcher informed Gorbachev. It can be safely assumed that the KGB was not happy about the news that one of their spies had been working for the West for a decade, but, as was their style, they stayed busy attempting to drive a wedge between London and Washington on nuclear testing and muddy the waters of the Gordievsky situation. The following month, the news of Gordievsky's defection became public, and in the ensuing war of words both sides expelled 25 nationals stationed in the opposite country.[80] It was an example of how the Cold War was still fully operational.

Meanwhile, the conflict in Afghanistan continued. Gorbachev was intent on withdrawing from a war he had never supported, and he attempted to transfer the responsibility for prosecuting the war to the Afghans themselves, with mixed results. By 1987, Gorbachev was actively looking for some kind of accord so that his forces could completely withdraw, which he did between 1987 and 1989. The war had been a propaganda disaster and was another reason the Americans could heavily criticize the Soviets at superpower summits. By making progress on ending the war, Gorbachev believed he might be in a stronger position on the broader geopolitical level.

An Acceleration of Domestic Policies

Early on, Gorbachev had introduced some policies marking a break with the past, but the results had not been what he hoped. Certainly, Glasnost allowed a level of dissent previously unheard of in the Soviet Union, and this more liberal approach to politics was a breath of fresh air in both the USSR and its satellite states in Central and Eastern Europe, but Perestroika had done little to revive the Soviet economy. In many areas the situation was grim. Ordinary Soviet citizens had to wait in queues for hours to get hold of even rudimentary items of food. Consumer goods were rare and choice was non-existent. Such was the economic slump in mid-late 1980s' Soviet Union. Moreover, the centrally planned economy suppressed the kind of prices signalling normal in a market economy. This manifested itself in a communist economy as shortages. It also meant that if the price mechanism was introduced, the economic situation would become much worse before it normalized, which is indeed what happened in the early 1990s. Problems were already visible by the end of 1987, and hardliners were becoming increasingly concerned about Glasnost and Perestroika, as well as foreign policy.

Gorbachev, however, had sufficient power to continue to make bold reforms, so Glasnost continued apace, even as the openness he had encouraged now fatally threatened the integrity of the Soviet Union itself.[81] The permissive environment of discussion allowed Soviet citizens to air

---

[79] Charles Moore, *Margaret Thatcher The Authorized Biography: Volume Two Everything She Wants* (Allen Lane, 2015), p. 263.
[80] Charles Moore, *Margaret Thatcher The Authorized Biography: Volume Two Everything She Wants* (Allen Lane, 2015), p. 265.

their grievances, and many of these cut to the core of the system. As historian Vladislav Zubok put it, Glasnost "discredited the entire foundation of Soviet foreign policy and the regime itself."[82] Gorbachev believed the criticism of his domestic policies was a sign he was not being radical enough. As a result, he pressed on further with Glasnost and Perestroika, and he sought to reform the structures of the communist party.

After decades of being repressed and silenced, Glasnost suddenly allowed Soviet citizens to speak their mind. For many, when they looked back on the period, this was the key change: the fear to speak out evaporated under Gorbachev's rule.[83] This began to show itself in unexpected ways. Riots had broken out in Kazakhstan in 1987, and Gorbachev interpreted the unrest to unresolved questions of nationality within the Soviet Union and sought to bring in some accountability, even democracy, to the political structures of his enormous country.[84] Unfortunately for Gorbachev, his approach did not go nearly far enough, which meant his changes would offer the prospect of more political power without really delivering. Nationalist demonstrations, independence movements, and even ethnic tensions in multiethnic countries like Yugoslavia would worsen during the following years, playing a major role in the dissolution of the USSR.

Part of Gorbachev's Perestroika had been the concept of *Uskoreniye,* or "acceleration." Essentially another slogan, Uskoreniye vaguely set out how Soviet industry needed to improve its processes, increase productivity, and generally modernize. However, in a sign that everything was not proceeding as intended, Gorbachev phased out Uskoreniye at the Communist Party Plenum of June 1987, instead refocusing his energy on a revamped Perestroika. In Gorbachev's view, the Soviet economy required more restructuring rather than acceleration, but this nuance was lost on many observers within the Soviet Union itself.

At the end of 1987, dissent from within the party came out into the open and a power struggle for the heart and soul of Soviet communism began. A leading figure in the army, General Dmitry Yazov, started criticizing Gorbachev's approach, claiming that the Soviet leader was damaging the prestige and honor of the country. The pressure from hardliners like Yazov and sympathetic members of the Politburo would increase until the failed coup of August 1991. Perhaps even more insidious became the pressure from liberal nationalist reformers, most notably Boris Yeltsin.

From the vantage point of the early 1980s, Gorbachev was a radical leader who found himself increasingly criticized by conservatives and liberals, the former for going too far, the latter for

---

[81] Vladislav M. Zubok, *Failed Empire: The Soviet Union in the Cold War from Stalin to Gorbachev* (The University of North Carolina Press, 2007), p. 309.

[82] Vladislav M. Zubok, *Failed Empire: The Soviet Union in the Cold War from Stalin to Gorbachev* (The University of North Carolina Press, 2007), p. 309.

[83] CNN, *Cold War* (TV Series, produced by Jeremy Isaacs and Pat Mitchell, 1998)

[84] Stephen White, *Communism and its Collapse* (Routledge, 2002), p. 77.

not going far enough. The liberals' most significant voice within the ruling elite was Boris Yeltsin, a Russian who came to represent a common trend within communist countries. Yeltsin wanted greater accountability, democracy, and reform, and in communist terms he was a liberal. When these principles were implemented, however, they often morphed into nationalist demands. Greater representation and nationalism were the forces that ultimately spelled doom for the Soviet Union.

Yeltsin had been appointed Mayor of Moscow in late 1985 and the following year was promoted to Politburo candidacy status itself. Shortly afterwards, Yeltsin began to criticize the Gorbachev regime for its lack of tangible reform. His key demand was more democratic accountability within the structures of the communist system.

Frustrated by the lack of progress, Yeltsin resigned from his positions and challenged Gorbachev at the Party Plenum in October 1987. The usually drab, tightly-managed plenum saw extraordinary scenes as Yeltsin took the stage to berate Gorbachev, who stood stunned close by. Gorbachev subsequently attacked Yeltsin's "immaturity" and took the opportunity to deepen his criticism at a party meeting in November, days after Yeltsin had been hospitalized. Yeltsin was demoted but would take his revenge on Gorbachev after the General Secretary had put in motion some of Yeltsin's actual demands.

Yeltsin

Tensions increased in the republics during this second phase of Gorbachev's leadership, and many of these disputes would culminate in civil wars as the USSR disintegrated and left a power vaccuum. One of the first to break out into the open was between the republics of Armenia and Azerbaijan. The focal point of the animosity between the two republics was the territory of Nagorno-Karabakh, then an autonomous "Oblast" within Azerbaijan. The population of Nagorno-Karabakh was mixed, with a majority of ethnic Armenians. Intoxicated by the new openness in the Soviet Union, the parliament of Nagorno-Karabakh voted to join the Armenian Soviet Republic in February 1988.[85] This set in motion a series of events that led to full-scale war, one that has still not been fully resolved.

The Azerbaijani regime fiercely resisted the move, requesting Moscow step in to reverse the decision, and ethnic violence took place between Armenians and Azerbaijanis as border clashes worsened.[86] Gorbachev sent in the Soviet army to put down the fighting, but even that ultimately failed. It was an extreme example of how a seemingly positive development, Glasnost, had lifted the lid on destructive sentiments such as nationalism, leading to the kind of ethnic violence that had not been seen for most of the USSR's existence.

Unrest emerged around the same time in the republics of Georgia, Ukraine, and Belarus, as well as the Baltic republics of Latvia, Lithuania, and Estonia. Moscow struggled to exert its will over the republics' increasingly angry populations.

Gorbachev believed he could circumvent these problems by providing more of a pressure valve for the grievances let loose by Glasnost. His major democratic reform was the establishment of the Congress of People's Deputies. Gorbachev secured party support for the Congress in July 1988 and went into action the following year. Over 2,000 deputies would sit in the Congress which would appoint key decision-making bodies for the USSR, such as the Supreme Soviet.

Although truly democratic, the Congress was nevertheless a huge departure from previous Soviet practice. Candidates for deputies were selected as members of public organizations, but there was some room for actual choice, which was unheard of in the USSR. Significantly, not all the candidates were Communist Party members, and perhaps even more significantly, the Congress elections permitted figures such as Boris Yeltsin to run, allowing him to make a major comeback. As a result of his election, Yeltsin was chosen by the Congress to take a seat on the Supreme Soviet, which was now the ultimate decision-making body of the USSR. This would bring Yeltsin back into direct confrontation with Gorbachev.

Crumbling Communism

Gorbachev and Reagan met again in Washington in December 1987, but a fundamental shift had taken place between the Reykjavik and Washington summits. Gorbachev's team had reason

---

[85] Thomas De Waal, *Black Garden: Armenia and Azerbaijan Through Peace and War* (CAP, 2003)
[86] Thomas De Waal, *Black Garden: Armenia and Azerbaijan Through Peace and War* (CAP, 2003)

to doubt the SDI would amount to much, and what had seemed so critical at the first two Reagan-Gorbachev meetings now appeared to be less important. The Soviets believed - rightly as it turned out - that SDI was little more than a bluff. Believing this, however, did not change the fact that Moscow desperately wanted to reduce its military spending and reduce its nuclear commitments.[87] Gorbachev knew that in this endeavour he had a willing partner in Reagan.

The result of the summit was the INF (Intermediate-Range Nuclear Forces) Treaty, which banned land-based short and medium range nuclear missiles, but not those launched by air or sea. A joint task force was established, and over the space of the next months and years, both sides did decommission thousands of these cruise missiles. It was a high point of the Reagan-Gorbachev collaboration.

For Gorbachev, the Washington trip was a resounding success and showed incontrovertibly that he was a completely different kind of Soviet leader. As his motorcade sped through downtown Washington, the Soviet leader spotted a waving crowd. Inexplicably for a communist leader, usually unaccustomed to public discussion, Gorbachev asked his driver to stop his car so that he could meet some of the crowd. Smiling, waving, and shaking hands, the Soviet Union was suddenly embodied by a personable, reasonable person. The stunt enhanced Gorbachev's status both in the United States and back at home, and the tension of the Cold War appeared to have been taken down several notches literally overnight. Gorbachev met a number of American journalists and even businesspeople on his trip, including a prominent New York real estate magnate named Donald Trump.[88]

After the 1987 summit, the USSR and US entered what can be considered a second era of détente. Tensions between the superpowers had significantly decreased, nuclear weapons were being decommissioned, and relations between the leaderships were warm. In fact, Gorbachev spent 1988 going further than the Americans could ever have imagined in reducing Cold War tensions. Reagan visited Moscow in 1988 shortly before leaving office, and at one point he was asked whether he still thought the Soviet Union was an "Evil Empire." As he said no, he put his arm around a beaming Gorbachev.[89]

Over the course of 1988, Gorbachev put in motion what came to be known as the "Sinatra Doctrine," which meant the countries in the Soviet Bloc would be able to choose their own path, and do things "their way."[90] In a sign of how Gorbachev had fundamentally misread the feelings of most of the people in the communist world, he thought that introducing democracy into these states, including his own, would present few problems because they would happily choose a

[87] CNN, *Cold War* (TV Series, produced by Jeremy Isaacs and Pat Mitchell, 1998)

[88] Maureen Dowd, "As 'Gorby' Works the Crowd, Backward Reels the K.G.B.," *The New York Times*, 11 December 1987, https://www.nytimes.com/1987/12/11/world/the-summit-as-gorby-works-the-crowd-backward-reels-the-kgb.html, [accessed 22 May 2019]

[89] CNN, *Cold War* (TV Series, produced by Jeremy Isaacs and Pat Mitchell, 1998)

[90] *The Irish Times*, "How Berlin's Wall came tumbling down," 1 November 1999, https://www.irishtimes.com/news/how-berlin-s-wall-came-tumbling-down-1.245060, [accessed 23 May 2019]

socialist system and socialist parties of their own volition.[91] This culminated in a famous speech Gorbachev made to the United Nations General Assembly on December 8, 1988. Gorbachev, even by his standards, shocked the world by announcing that he would withdraw many - although not all - Soviet troops from Central and Eastern Europe.[92] He also asserted that Moscow would not interfere in the domestic affairs of these communist states.[93] Gorbachev vowed to "expand the Soviet Union's participation in the United Nations and Conference of Security and Cooperation in Europe human rights monitoring arrangements," and that "implementation of agreements on human rights should be binding on all states."[94] This was quite a departure for the leader of an authoritarian, communist state.

In *Gorbachev and the German Question: Soviet-West German Relations, 1985-1990*, author David Shumaker argued that Hungary's leaders, though desirous of encouraging a thaw, consistently communicated with Moscow, asking permission even as late as the summer of 1989 as to what to do about the thousands of East Germans fleeing the country through Hungary's borders.[95] Additionally, Shumaker notes, if the Soviet Union desired in any way to stop the crescendoing protest movement, Gorbachev could have used force or declaration of martial law to do so, even as late as 1989. Shumaker concluded, "Did the Soviet leader labor under the grand illusion of communism's inevitable triumph in Eastern Europe? Or alternatively, had Gorbachev already accepted the SED's imminent and total failure? In all likelihood, Gorbachev's reasoning lay somewhere between these two extremes."[96]

Around the same time, Gorbachev also negotiated an end to the war in Afghanistan, having wound down the conflict gradually since his rise to power. Before his speech to the UN, an agreement was reached in Geneva on April 14, 1988. Soviet Foreign Minister Shevardnadze signed the accords that ended the conflict, along with signatories from Afghanistan and Pakistan as well as US Secretary of State George Shultz.[97] The Soviets began pulling out their troops from Afghanistan in May 1988, taking until February 1989 to withdraw the last of its military.[98]

---

[91] CNN, *Cold War* (TV Series, produced by Jeremy Isaacs and Pat Mitchell, 1998)

[92] *History*, "Perestroika and Glasnost," 21 August 2018, https://www.history.com/topics/cold-war/perestroika-and-glasnost, [accessed 23 May 2019]

[93] *The New York Times*, "The Gorbachev Visit; Excerpts From Speech to U.N. on Major Soviet Military Cuts," 8 December 1988, https://www.nytimes.com/1988/12/08/world/the-gorbachev-visit-excerpts-from-speech-to-un-on-major-soviet-military-cuts.html, [accessed 23 May 2019}

[94] *The New York Times*, "The Gorbachev Visit; Excerpts From Speech to U.N. on Major Soviet Military Cuts," 8 December 1988, https://www.nytimes.com/1988/12/08/world/the-gorbachev-visit-excerpts-from-speech-to-un-on-major-soviet-military-cuts.html, [accessed 23 May 2019}

[95] David H. Shumaker, Gorbachev and the German Question: Soviet-West German Relations, 1985-1990 (Westport, CT: Praeger Publishers, 1995), 105, https://www.questia.com/read/27983284.

[96] Ibid 107.

[97] Rosanne Klass, "Afghanistan: The Accords," *Foreign Affairs*, 1988, https://www.foreignaffairs.com/articles/asia/1988-06-01/afghanistan-accords, [accessed 23 May 2019]

[98] Franz-Stefan Gady, "30-Year Anniversary of Soviet Withdrawal From Afghanistan: A Successful Disengagement Operation?," *The Diplomat*, 6 February 2019, https://thediplomat.com/2019/02/30-year-anniversary-of-soviet-withdrawal-from-afghanistan-a-successful-disengagement-operation/, [accessed 23 May 2019]

This marked another successful initiative for Gorbachev, but the country had been devastated by a decade of war and was divided into numerous factions. Fighting resumed shortly after the Soviet withdrawal, and after years of further conflict, the Taliban came to power in 1996, providing refuge for the al-Qaeda terrorist group. Both the Taliban and al-Qaeda had some connections with the US-funded mujahideen fighting the Soviets in the 1980s. Scholars used the term "blowback" to describe the long-term impact of the Cold War into the 2000s after the US and its allies invaded Afghanistan in the wake of the 9/11 attacks.[99]

Nevertheless, all these moves seemed to that Gorbachev was a man who stuck by his commitments and was someone keen to reduce the tension and proxy conflicts of the Cold War. He visited a number of communist states in 1989, encouraging their leaders to follow his lead on Glasnost and Perestroika. He was known to find a couple of these particularly frustrating, such as Romania's dictator Nicolae Ceaușescu and East German communist leader Erich Honecker. Gorbachev was apparently shocked by the dire state of Romania, with its paucity of goods and the desperate state of its people.[100] He also visited China in May 1989 to mend relations with Beijing after decades of tension during the Sino-Soviet split, and he became the first Soviet leader to visit China for almost 30 years. Nevertheless, his visit coincided with the Tiananmen Square student protests, which were violently crushed after Gorbachev left.

Gorbachev's openness meant that he would go so far as to entertain criticism of his East German ally from a West Germen leader, in the case of a conversation held between him and Helmut Kohl of West Germany in June of 1989. Kohl complained to Gorbachev, "Now a couple of words about our mutual friends. I will tell you directly that Erich Honecker concerns me a great deal. His wife has just made a statement, in which she called on East German youth to take up arms and, if necessary, defend the achievements of socialism against external enemies. She clearly implied that socialist countries which implement reforms, stimulate democratic processes, and follow their own original road, are enemies. Primarily, she had Poland and Hungary in mind."[101]

---

[99] Chalmers Johnson, *Blowback: The Costs and Consequences of American Empire*, (Holt, 2004)

[100] Celestine Bohlen, 'Gorbachev challenged by Romania', *The Washington Post*, 28 May 1987, https://www.washingtonpost.com/archive/politics/1987/05/28/gorbachev-challenged-by-romania/39020705-b8eb-470c-9244-e98f4257ce97/?utm_term=.823b4c8dafb3, [accessed 14 November 2018]

[101] William Taubman and Svetlana Savranskaya, "Chapter 3: If a Wall Fell in Berlin and Moscow Hardly Noticed, Would It Still Make a Noise?," in The Fall of the Berlin Wall: The Revolutionary Legacy of 1989, ed. Jeffrey A. Engel (New York: Oxford University Press, 2009), 85, https://www.questia.com/read/121390201.

Kohl in 1989

The Soviet leader also had an uncomfortable meeting with the Warsaw Pact leaders later that year. Changes were happening rapidly in Central and Eastern Europe by mid-1989, and a peaceful transition to liberal democracy appeared to be taking place in Hungary and Poland. This seriously concerned the likes of Honecker and Ceaușescu, who wanted Gorbachev to intervene and w worried the demand for reform would spread to their countries. This proved to be correct, and it had much deeper ramifications than anyone could have imagined.

Just a few short and hectic months later, Gorbachev would head to East Germany to visit his and Chancellor Kohl's "mutual friends". On October 6-7, 1989, East Berlin was to celebrate the 40th anniversary of the founding of the East German state, but security and surveillance by the Stasi had been increased heavily in response to Honecker's concerns that the visit of the Soviet leader, Gorbachev could cause unrest in the city. Gorbachev's very controlled visit did spark local protests, though he did not openly call for reform in a way that would make the East German leadership uncomfortable. He did, however, in his meeting with the leaders of the Socialist party give a warning that "one cannot overlook signals of reality. Life punishes those who arrive too late. We have learned this from our development".[102] Shumaker argues, though, that Gorbachev did the most he could to make the point that he supported national sovereignty: "During his stay in East Berlin for the 40th anniversary of the East German state, Gorbachev

---

[102] Gorbachev qtd. in Shumaker 112.

publicly stressed that 'in each country the people will determine what they need and what to do'."[103] Behind the scenes, Honecker defended his hard line attitude to Gorbachev, reminding him that the East Germans boasted a higher standard of living than the citizens of the Soviet Union. If East Germany lost the ability to retain its young people, Honecker warned, East Germany's reputation and her high-tech generation would be lost to unrest and exodus.

According to Valery Boldin, a former Gorbachev aide, when Gorbachev returned from East Germany, he "announced that Honecker's days were numbered and that we should start thinking about the reunification of Germany".[104] On October 16th, Egon Krenz and two other East German leaders, Willi Stoph and Erich Mielke, wrote to Moscow seeking Gorbachev's permission to replace Honecker as leader. Honecker would be removed from office only a few days later.[105]

Observers in the Soviet Union described Gorbachev's approach to the situation in Europe as "ad hoc". According to observers , Gorbachev and his minister of Soviet affairs were "[a]ble but inexperienced, impatient to reach agreement, but excessively self-assured and flattered by the Western media... often outwitted and outplayed by their Western partners".[106] History records no direct comment on the fall of the wall by Gorbachev, whose own aides found him unable to be reached by phone on the night of November 9th. That said, in 2009, 20 years after the Wall fell Gorbachev did make comments to Western reporters about the Berlin Wall: "If the Soviet Union did not want [the wall to fall], nothing would have happened, not any kind of unification." When asked what the alternative would be, Gorbachev answered, "I don't know, maybe a World War III...I am very proud of the decision we made. The wall did not simply fall, it was destroyed, just as the Soviet Union was destroyed...The fall of the Berlin Wall was a synthesized indication of what was going on in the world and where it was heading to. My policy was open and sincere, a policy aimed at using democracy and not spilling blood, but this cost me very [dearly], I can tell you that."[107]

When Gorbachev decided it was time for Honecker to exit the scene, the Politburo had already decided on his replacement, a younger man, to be sure, but a man embroiled in the same fight as his unfortunate predecessor. Egon Krenz had grown up in the Soviet system, attending college and becoming known as the "crown prince" of the GDR for his faithfulness in matters of party security .[108] He replaced his mentor and friend Honecker, the man he called his "foster father

[103] Ibid 106.

[104] Valery Boldin, Ten Years That Shook the World: The Gorbachev Era as Witnessed by His Chief of Staff, trans. Evelyn Rossiter (New York: Basic Books, 1994), 143,

[105] Large, 525.

[106] Vladislav M. Zubok, A Failed Empire: The Soviet Union in the Cold War from Stalin to Gorbachev (Chapel Hill, NC: University of North Carolina Press, 2007), 327,

[107] Marquardt, Alexander. "Gorbachev: The Man Who Prevented World War III?" ABC News.com. 8 November 2009.

[108] Dennis Kavanagh, ed., A Dictionary of Political Biography (Oxford: Oxford University Press, 1998), 276, https://www.questia.com

and political teacher", after betraying him and voting for his ouster in the midst of Honecker's disagreements with the Soviets and failures to control the burgeoning protest movement in East Germany. Krenz, however, did not have the trust of the people any more than Honecker had at the end of his rule. An exiled East German said Krenz was "a walking invitation to flee the republic".[109] Stern calls Krenz "a less doctrinaire functionary [than Honecker] mouthing vague notions of reform".[110]

Krenz, who unluckily received the ailing Honecker's "blessing" upon his exit, proved paralyzed and unable to deal with the demands for reform. Krenz lost popularity by taking over not only as the Socialist party leader but also as head of state, the same position which Honecker had occupied.[111] Despite Krenz's desperate attempts to placate reformers in East Germany, his promises proved too little, too late. He was seen as nothing more than Honecker "with a gallbladder", as the joke went. The number of protestors in Leipzig grew during Krenz's first six weeks in power from 70,000 to over half a million, and Krenz opened the borders with Czechoslovakia on the advice of the Soviets only after he revealed to Gorbachev the extreme amount of debt East Germany had incurred with the West. Krenz and Gorbachev knew they would need to build good will with the West in order to make the payments necessary for the GR to survive.[112]

Finally, tensions between East Germany and her resentful neighbors had reached a breaking point. With literally tens of thousands of East German refugees clogging the streets, highways, and embassies of her neighbor nations, it was up to East Germany to ease travel restrictions and make some concessions to stem the tide, so the decision was made to allow travel outside of East Berlin for one month to those with proper passports. Large notes that the number of East Germans with proper passports was so low that this would not have caused a high influx of travel outside of the borders. However, the hastily called press conference and the rewriting of the policy up to the last hour meant that a mistake would be made that would change the world as the Germans knew it.

Guenter Schabowski was the official spokesperson at a press conference that was being televised live throughout East Germany. Charged with delivering the new travel guidelines in a hastily-called press conference, Schabowski began his remarks: "You see, comrades, I was informed today…that such an announcement had been…distributed earlier today. You should actually have it already…1) 'Applications for travel abroad by private individuals can now be made without the previously existing requirements (of demonstrating a need to travel or proving familial relationships). The travel authorizations will be issued within a short time. Grounds for denial will only be applied in particular exceptional cases. The responsible departments of

---

[109] Ibid. 526.
[110] Stern 457.
[111] Kavanagh 276.
[112] Vladislav M. Zubok, A Failed Empire: The Soviet Union in the Cold War from Stalin to Gorbachev (Chapel Hill, NC: University of North Carolina Press, 2007), 326

passport and registration control in the People's Police district offices in the GDR are instructed to issue visas for permanent exit without delays and without presentation of the existing requirements for permanent exit.""

After being asked when it would come into effect, Schabowski replied, "That comes into effect, according to my information, immediately, without delay." When asked if it also applies for West Berlin, he responded, "Permanent exit can take place via all border crossings from the GDR to the FRG and West Berlin, respectively."[113]

Picture of the press conference

The Wall Street Journal speculated that Schabowski had faltered not because he had not prepared carefully enough, as some charged, but because he was "not used to scrutiny by a free press...[And] he couldn't deal with rapid-fire questions from international journalists".[114] Whatever the real cause of Schabowski's struggle to communicate, it became immediately clear that "seeming accidents have the power to shape history".[115] Later, American journalist Tom

---

[113] Guenter Schabowski, "Guenter Schabowski's Press Conference in the GDR International Press Center," Making the History of 1989, Item #449, http://chnm.gmu.edu/1989/items/show/449 (accessed February 27 2015, 8:28 pm).

[114] Walker, Marcus. "Did Journalists' Questions Topple the Berlin Wall?" The Wall Street Journal. 7 November 2014.

[115] Stern 459.

Brokaw would recall following Schakowsky upstairs after the conference had concluded and asking him to re-read the portion of the brief that lifted the travel restrictions on border crossings between East and West Berlin directly. It was then, Brokaw realized, that the end of the Berlin Wall had come. In his newscast, he told the watching world, "This is a historic night…. The East German Government has just declared that East German citizens will be able to cross the wall … without restrictions."[116] Schabowski would be expelled from the party but fail to escape prosecution as a high Politburo official; he served only a few months of a three-year sentence after distancing himself from communist ideals.

On the evening of November 9, 1989, Harald Jaeger, an East German border guard, watched a television as he ate a meal at the canteen before arriving for his guard duty shift at the Berlin Wall that night at 6:00 p.m. Hearing the removal of travel restrictions would take place "immediately", he remembers "almost choking on my bread roll". He arrived at the wall to find other skeptical guards and made multiple telephone calls to his superiors, attempting to get clarification about what to do with the now gathering crowds. At first, Jaeger's superiors simply ignored his question, telling them to send people without authorization home. After realizing the seriousness of the situation, however, Jaeger was instructed to let the "most agitated" members of the crowd pass through to West Berlin in hopes of appeasing them. Obviously, the opposite effect was achieved and Jaeger had no further instruction from his superiors. Fearing for the safety of the burgeoning crowd, Jaeger delivered the order to open the border between East and West Berlin at 11:30 p.m.[117] Thus, Jaeger is most often credited with being the man who actually "took down" the Berlin Wall.

Another East German border guard, Erich Wittman, recalled his memory of the evening: "I was promoted to Corporal, and was directly posted as the Officer of the main checkpoint of the Berlin wall. I still remember the tensions, thousands of cars was in front of me, honking and wanted me to move, which I refused….The news of the Berlin wall being open for anyone hadn't reached us who were posted at the wall, only when my girlfriend, who I for the first time on [sic] months seen, came to me and told me about it. I was in shock and didn't know what to do, all around me, thousands of people started to gather around me, climbing over the wall, some even brought tools and sledge-hammers and started to destroy the wall, the people kept yelling at us as we told them to stay back, then…On the TV, which I saw through the window of the Guard's Resting place, I could see the politicians ordering the opening to West Berlin for everyone, I ordered the soldiers to open the gates and let the cars pass, the yells formed into cheers and all over us, people came to hug me and my men, and the cars kept swarming over the border. Erika grabbed onto my uniform, and pulled me to her, and hugged me, I responded in kissing her, then a camera man appeared on the scene and filmed the opening of the wall, and got us on tape…The

---

[116] Melvyn P. Leffler, "Chapter 5: Dreams of Freedom, Temptations of Power," in The Fall of the Berlin Wall: The Revolutionary Legacy of 1989, ed. Jeffrey A. Engel (New York: Oxford University Press, 2009), 136,

[117] "Former border guard Harald Jaeger recalls how he opened the Berlin Wall." South China Morning Post. 6 November 2014.

supreme officer came to me later, asked me why the people are flooding over to West Germany, I told him. The German Democratic Republic is dead, they announced it on Television, open your borders as well for these people. He quickly went away, and all over East Germany the news came, and the Berlin wall was flooded by people over several days."

A crane removing pieces of the wall in December 1989

Pictures of East Germans talking to West Germans through the wall in late November 1989

1990 picture of the graffiti and pieces of the wall chipped away

A New World Order

The world had been taken by surprise when the Berlin Wall came down, and Kohl wasted no time in asserting himself regarding the situation. On November 28, Kohl gave a speech setting out "Ten Points" that would lead to greater German cooperation, and eventually even reunification.[118] The concessions made in the 1972 Basic Treaty had apparently been forgotten, and the pre-1972 policy of incorporating the whole of Germany within one democratic state was

---

[118] The German Chancellery, 'The Federal Chancellor, Helmut Kohl; 1982-1998', [accessed 31 October 2017], https://www.bundeskanzlerin.de/Webs/BKin/EN/Chancellery/Timeline_Federal_Chancellors_since_1949/Kohl/kohl_node.html, Robert Hutchings, 'American Diplomacy and the End of the Cold War in Europe', *Foreign Policy Breakthroughs: Cases in Successful Diplomacy*, ed. Robert Hutchings and Jeremi Suri (Oxford: Oxford University Press, 2015, pp. 148-172), p. 160.

back on the table.

Though Kohl's objectives appeared ambitious, it was thought the Soviets would not accept a unified Germany as part of NATO, and two of West Germany's closest allies, Britain and France, were opposed to unification, fearing Germany might try to dominate Europe as it had attempted to do in the first half of the 20th century. Margaret Thatcher, in an interview outside 10 Downing Street, warned that talk of German reunification was much, much "too fast" and that East Germany would be required to show its development as a democracy before that could be taken under serious consideration. Despite issuing cautions about the pace at which reunification should take place and the idea that it was impossible for all East Germans to leave the country[119], Thatcher did take a moment to delight in the historical moment: "I think it is a great day for freedom. I watched the scenes on television last night and again this morning because I felt one ought not only hear about them but see them because you see the joy on people's faces and you see what freedom means to them; it makes you realize that you cannot stifle or suppress people's desire for liberty and so I watched with the same joy as everyone else."[120]

Meanwhile, President George H.W. Bush was determined to use American influence to bring a peaceful end to the Cold War and forge a durable, pro-Western settlement in Europe. He was assisted by the fact that his administration had good working relations with Gorbachev and other Soviet officials, such as Foreign Minister Shevardnadze. As a result, an environment of mutual trust, or at least good faith, existed between Moscow and Washington in 1990. The Bush administration also realized that Gorbachev was coming under increasing pressure from his own hardliners, as well as liberal reformers such as Boris Yeltsin and nationalist agitators in the Soviet republics.

The US was keen to support Gorbachev and prevent a chaotic breakup of the USSR, with the exception of the Baltic states (Latvia, Lithuania and Estonia), which had been incorporated into the Soviet Union at the end of the Second World War. Many of the people occupying the Baltic republics bitterly opposed Soviet rule, and as the communist regimes toppled in rapid succession in Europe, separatist movements saw their opportunity. The independence-minded populations in the Baltic republics formed "Popular Fronts" in the late 1980s, with Estonia declaring sovereignty in 1988 and Latvia and Lithuania following in the summer of 1989. In August 1989, protestors in the three republics formed a human chain across their territory, known as the "Baltic Way." The protest marked the 50th anniversary of the Hitler-Stalin pact non-aggression pact that prevented immediate hostilities between the Nazis and Soviets in the Second World War but set the Baltic countries on course for occupation by both dictatorships. On March 11, 1990, the Lithuanian parliament declared independence, drawing an uncertain response from Moscow. In the interim period, Latvia and Estonia also declared independence before the Red

---

[119] Thatcher, Margaret. "Remarks on the Berlin Wall (fall thereof)". Thatcher Archive: COI transcript. 10 November 1989.
[120] Ibid.

Army attempted, dramatically, to reassert Soviet sovereignty.

In one of the darkest moments of Gorbachev's premiership, he sent the Soviet army into Lithuania to take back control from the separatists in early 1991. Known as the "January Events," the Lithuanians resisted the Soviet army in the capital city, Vilnius. 14 Lithuanians died and 700 were injured before the Soviet army retreated, and Gorbachev was heavily criticized for the move. The Lithuanians, although overjoyed after having pushed back the Red Army, were furious with Gorbachev's actions, even as just about everyone understood the violence would have been far worse under a different Soviet leader.[121] It may be that Gorbachev finally saw the writing on the wall, that his country was facing an existential crisis, or that he had come under heavy pressure from military hawks and hardliners. Ultimately, though, the Soviets essentially conceded the independence of the Baltic states, and in a few short years they would be part of NATO and the EU.

Gorbachev experienced a strange duality in 1990 and 1991. He was feted on the international scene for his role in ending Soviet domination in Central and Eastern Europe and allowing these states to make a peaceful transition away from communism. The international arena was transformed, with the Soviet Union suddenly acting virtually in concert with the United States. At home, however, the USSR was in turmoil, and Gorbachev was apparently powerless to prevent his country's dissolution.

In August 1990, Iraqi dictator Saddam Hussein invaded tiny, oil-rich Kuwait, and President Bush quickly put together a broad-based coalition of countries with the goal of forcing the Iraqis out of Kuwait. Bush put pressure on Iraq and eventually obtained permission to use military force against the Iraqis through the United Nations Security Council. After months of sanctions, "Operation Desert Storm" achieved a quick victory against Hussein and forced the Iraqi forces from Kuwait in early 1991. Gorbachev acquiesced to a number of American resolutions in the UN throughout this time, most notably those on Iraq.[122]

The US and USSR also worked together on the Middle East peace process. Bush convened the Madrid Peace Conference in October and November 1991, an attempt to bring together the hostile parties in the Middle East and figure out a solution to the Palestinian-Israeli conflict. Gorbachev was in attendance and threw his support behind the process. Again, what was different about this move was that traditionally the US and Soviet Union had used the region as a proxy for their broader conflict. Various states and factions had received support from either the Americans or Soviets, and sometimes both. A united front from Bush and Gorbachev changed the calculus for many leaders in the region, not least the Israelis.

---

[121] Witold Janczys and Markian Ostaptschuk, "The January bloodbath in Lithuania 25 years on," *Deutsche Welle*, 13 January 2016, https://www.dw.com/en/the-january-bloodbath-in-lithuania-25-years-on/a-18976152, [accessed 24 May 2019]

[122] Graham E. Fuller, "Moscow and the Gulf War," *Foreign Affairs*, Summer 1991, https://www.foreignaffairs.com/articles/russia-fsu/1991-06-01/moscow-and-gulf-war, [accessed 24 May 2019]

Nevertheless, by late 1991 Gorbachev's authority was fading fast. Although still a statesman on the world stage, his own country was in turmoil. Georgians had taken to the streets in April 1989, demanding secession from the Soviet Union and the incorporation of the disputed territory of Abkhazia. Soviet troops cracked down on the demonstrators, killing 20 people. An anti-Georgian riot broke out in Abkhazia soon afterwards, marking the start of a conflict between Abkhazians and Georgians that would stretch into the 1990s.

A similar situation emerged in Moldova. The Romanian-speaking population agitated for independence from the USSR during 1989, and another "Popular Front" formed. Some Moldovans even wanted to join Romania itself. This was opposed, however, by the pro-Russian population in the eastern region of Transnistria, which led to another conflict that is still unresolved nearly 30 years later.

Nationalist demonstrations also broke out in Ukraine, Belarus, Kazakhstan, and Uzbekistan, and in several cases Moscow sent in troops to quell the disturbances. Azerbaijan's "Black January" came when Soviet troops attempted to retain control of the republic and in the process killed 130 people.

Six republics declared independence in 1990, including Moldova, Georgia, and Armenia, but it was clear the real danger to the integrity of the USSR would come if its largest republics - Russia and Ukraine - attempted to break away. Russia held its first democratic elections in June 1991, with Boris Yeltsin emerging victorious with 57% of the vote. The Soviet Union was a fragile edifice rapidly losing the consent of its constituent republics, and Russia now wanted to reformulate the USSR as a federation of independent states, loosening the grip of the Soviet Union.

In a final, desperate attempt to prevent the implosion of the USSR, a group of hardliners launched a coup. On August 19, 1991, the Soviet plotters - including Defense Minister Dmitry Yazov and KBG leader Vladimir Kryuchkov - visited Gorbachev at his holiday dacha in Crimea and attempted something along the same lines as in a previous era, such as the defenestration of Nikita Khrushchev in 1964. They told the 60-year-old Gorbachev that he would retire due to health reasons and then proceeded to make a preposterous announcement on Soviet television about a change of leadership.

The coup was clear for all to see. Boris Yeltsin stormed down to the Russian parliament, demanding the coup plotters step down and reinstate Gorbachev. The plotters blinked on August 21 upon realizing their takeover had little support either in the corridors of power or in the country at large.

Gorbachev was reinstated and back in office, but his power was almost gone. In the months after the coup, 10 former Soviet republics declared their independence, and a transitional confederation known as the Commonwealth of Independent States (CIS) was put in place, intending to allow a looser version of the Soviet Union to continue. This became a reality after a meeting between the leaders of Russia (Yeltsin), Ukraine (Leonid Kravchuk) and Belarus (Stanislav Shushkevich) on December 8, 1991. The so-called "Belovezha Accords," named after the location in Belarus where they were signed, effectively withdrew the three countries from the USSR and declared the Soviet Union dissolved.

There has been some debate as to whether the leaders had the authority to do this. After all, Gorbachev was still the head of the USSR, but nevertheless it was clear where real power now existed. Yeltsin was the most important political leader in the region after the failed August coup, and the accords would establish a new Russian Federation which he would lead until the end of the decade. Gorbachev initially rejected the assertions of the Belovezha Accords but quickly faced the new reality and yielded. On December 25, 1991, Gorbachev announced in a television address that he would resign and the Soviet Union would be dissolved at the end of the year. After 74 years of communist experiment, the Soviet Union was no more, and the Cold War was over.

It has often been said that Mikhail Gorbachev was far more popular in the West than in his native Russia. Having overseen the relatively peaceful end of the Cold War and domination of communism in Central and Eastern Europe, Gorbachev's domestic policies led remorselessly to the downfall of the Soviet Union itself. By 1992, the Soviet Union had been transformed into 15 independent states, and for most of these new states, the 1990s proved to be worse than the previous decade. Some experienced civil war, and breakaway provinces such as Chechnya went through bloody conflicts in their attempts to gain independence. Many of these conflicts are still unresolved.

The economies of these states were also heavily damaged. Prices soared while goods remained scarce, and Russia experienced a humiliating default and devaluation of the rouble currency in 1998. Many of these states continued in the authoritarian tradition, as democracy proved very difficult to embed. In the worst examples, former communist party bosses were effectively made autocrats for life. Resources were fiercely fought over during the 1990s - encouraged by liberals in the West, the former Soviet states implemented an unrestrained version of capitalism, with chaotic and mismanaged privatizations and economic reforms. The phenomenon of the ultra-rich "oligarch" emerged during this period, and ultimately, Vladimir Putin restored some semblance of order to Russia after he came to power in late 1999 and revived the Russian economy as the country benefitted from a commodity price boom.

How much of this legacy was due to the policies of the Gorbachev regime remains a much-debated question. Several of his reforms led to far-reaching, unpredictable consequences, and it is probably fair to say that most other Soviet leaders would not have relinquished the Warsaw Pact states without a fight in 1989. In this respect, Gorbachev's generally peaceable approach and his humane outlook allowed these upheavals to take place without as much bloodshed.

Of course, while those affected will be debating the rights and wrongs of Gorbachev's decisions for decades to come, what cannot be argued is the significance of his leadership.

Online Resources

Other books about 20th century history by Charles River Editors

Other books about Russian history by Charles River Editors

Other books about Brezhnev on Amazon

Bibliography

Christopher Andrew and Vasili Mitrokhin, *The Mitrokhin Archive: The KGB in Europe and the West*, (Gardners Books, 2000)

Edwin Bacon & Mark Sandle, *Brezhnev Reconsidered* (Palgrave Macmillan, 2002)

S.J. Ball, *The Cold War: An International History 1947-1991* (London: Arnold, 1998)

Celestine Bohlen, 'Gorbachev challenged by Romania', *The Washington Post*, 28 May 1987, https://www.washingtonpost.com/archive/politics/1987/05/28/gorbachev-challenged-by-romania/39020705-b8eb-470c-9244-e98f4257ce97/?utm_term=.823b4c8dafb3

Archie Brown, *The Gorbachev Factor* (Oxford University Press, 1996)

John Campbell, *Margaret Thatcher Volume Two: The Iron Lady* (Random House, 2003)

CNN, *Cold War* (TV Series, produced by Jeremy Isaacs and Pat Mitchell, 1998)

Thomas De Waal, *Black Garden: Armenia and Azerbaijan Through Peace and War* (CAP, 2003)

Maureen Dowd, "As 'Gorby' Works the Crowd, Backward Reels the K.G.B.," *The New York Times*, 11 December 1987, https://www.nytimes.com/1987/12/11/world/the-summit-as-gorby-works-the-crowd-backward-reels-the-kgb.html

Stan Fedun, 'How Alcohol Conquered Russia', *The Atlantic*, 25 September 2003, https://www.theatlantic.com/international/archive/2013/09/how-alcohol-conquered-russia/279965/

Graham E. Fuller, "Moscow and the Gulf War," *Foreign Affairs*, Summer 1991, https://www.foreignaffairs.com/articles/russia-fsu/1991-06-01/moscow-and-gulf-war

Mary Fulbrook, *History of Germany, 1918-2000: the divided nation* (Oxford: Blackwell, 2002)

Franz-Stefan Gady, "30-Year Anniversary of Soviet Withdrawal From Afghanistan: A Successful Disengagement Operation?," *The Diplomat*, 6 February 2019, https://thediplomat.com/2019/02/30-year-anniversary-of-soviet-withdrawal-from-afghanistan-a-successful-disengagement-operation/

The German Chancellery, 'The Federal Chancellor, Helmut Kohl; 1982-1998', [accessed 31 October 2017], https://www.bundeskanzlerin.de/Webs/BKin/EN/Chancellery/Timeline_Federal_Chancellors_since_1949/Kohl/kohl_node.html

Mark Gilbert, *Cold War Europe: The Politics of a Contested Continent* (Rowman & Littlefield, 2014)

History, "Perestroika and Glasnost," 21 August 2018, https://www.history.com/topics/cold-war/perestroika-and-glasnost

Godfrey Hodgson, *People's Century: From the dawn of the century to the eve of the millennium* (Godalming: BBC Books, 1998)

Robert Hutchings, 'American Diplomacy and the End of the Cold War in Europe', *Foreign Policy Breakthroughs: Cases in Successful Diplomacy*, ed. Robert Hutchings and Jeremi Suri (Oxford: Oxford University Press, 2015, pp. 148-172)

The Irish Times, "How Berlin's Wall came tumbling down," 1 November 1999, https://www.irishtimes.com/news/how-berlin-s-wall-came-tumbling-down-1.245060

Witold Janczys and Markian Ostaptschuk, "The January bloodbath in Lithuania 25 years on," *Deutsche Welle*, 13 January 2016, https://www.dw.com/en/the-january-bloodbath-in-lithuania-25-years-on/a-18976152

Chalmers Johnson, *Blowback: The Costs and Consequences of American Empire*, (Holt, 2004)

Rosanne Klass, "Afghanistan: The Accords," *Foreign Affairs*, 1988, https://www.foreignaffairs.com/articles/asia/1988-06-01/afghanistan-accords

Michael McFaul, *Russia's Unfinished Revolution: Political Change from Gorbachev to Putin* (Cornell University Press, 2002)

Charles Moore, *Margaret Thatcher The Authorized Biography: Volume Two Everything She Wants* (Allen Lane, 2015)

"The Gorbachev Visit; Excerpts From Speech to U.N. on Major Soviet Military Cuts," *The New York Times*, 8 December 1988, https://www.nytimes.com/1988/12/08/world/the-gorbachev-visit-excerpts-from-speech-to-un-on-major-soviet-military-cuts.html

Arkady Ostrovsky, *The Invention of Russia: The Journey from Gorbachev's Freedom to Putin's War* (Atlantic Books, 2015)

William Taubman, *Gorbachev: His Life and Times*. New York City: Simon and Schuster, 2017)

Margaret Thatcher, *The Downing Street Years* (Harper Collins, 1993)

William J. Tompson, *The Soviet Union under Brezhnev*, (Routledge, 2014).

Peter Wensierski, 'Die WG der Rebellen', *Der Spiegel*, 3 October 2014, http://www.spiegel.de/einestages/leipzig-wie-es-1989-zur-montagsdemonstration-kam-a-993513.html

Stephen White, *Communism and its Collapse* (Routledge, 2002)

Tom Wicker, "The Zero Option Revived," *The New York Times*, 4 March 1987, https://www.nytimes.com/1987/03/04/opinion/in-the-nation-the-zero-option-revived.html

Vladislav M. Zubok, *Failed Empire: The Soviet Union in the Cold War from Stalin to Gorbachev* (The University of North Carolina Press, 2007)

Free Books by Charles River Editors

We have brand new titles available for free most days of the week. To see which of our titles are currently free, click on this link.

Discounted Books by Charles River Editors

We have titles at a discount price of just 99 cents everyday. To see which of our titles are currently 99 cents, click on this link.